Czech

The Czech Book

Revised and Expanded

RECIPES • HISTORY • FOLK ARTS
NORTH AMERICAN CZECHS COAST TO COAST

Saint Ludmila with Saint Wenceslaus
St. Wenceslaus Church, Cedar Rapids, Iowa

by **Pat Martin**

Dedication

Dedicated to the millions of Americans who celebrate their status with *Czech Touches!* May you continue to learn about and understand your cultural heritage and share it with others who also have personal stories of identity, family, community, and purposeful lives in this great country.

Front cover: Amanda De Hoedt served as Miss Czech-Slovak Iowa and represented the state at the national Miss Czech-Slovak U.S. Pageant at the Czech Festival in Wilber, Nebraska. Amanda (whose mother is a Netolicky) earned a BS in bio-medical engineering at the University of Iowa. While pursuing her MS, Amanda worked in the Republic of Ghana in West Africa on a civil engineering management project to erect a water tower and distribution system. As part of her studies, Amanda has traveled to Egypt, the Czech Republic, Romania, the Philippines, and Costa Rica. Her father, Russ De Hoedt, photographed her for the cover of this book.

Back Cover: The St. Paul Czech and Slovak dancers

Title Page: St. Wenceslaus with St. Ludmila sculpture
Photograph by John Johnson

In 1904, the center of religious and social life in Cedar Rapids, Iowa, was St. Wenceslaus Catholic Church, Czech National Parish. Hand built by parishioners, it became a hub of southeast Cedar Rapids. To celebrate the centennial of this historic church in 2004, the adjoining St. Wenceslaus Czech Heritage Park was created. The centerpiece of the park is an exact replica of the fourteen-foot-high St. Wenceslaus with St. Ludmila statuary that is showcased on the Charles Bridge in Prague, Czech Republic.

The statue depicts St. Wenceslaus as a young child, being taught the Bible by his grandmother, St. Ludmila. This statue was commissioned by St. Wenceslaus Parish and sculpted in the Czech Republic by Czech artist Jan Kotek. The National Czech & Slovak Museum & Library in Cedar Rapids and the National Czech Museum in Prague cooperated in obtaining the original model from which the statue was created. The artist accompanied his work to Cedar Rapids and presided over its placement.

Acknowledgements see page 127.

To view all titles available go to: www.penfieldbooks.com.
Join us on Facebook at: www.facebook.com/penfield.books for the latest updates.

©2012 Penfield Books ISBN-13: 9781932043556
Library of Congress Control Number: 2012945379   Printed in the U.S.A.

Contents

The Czech Lands: Dates in History

A.D. 500 The Romans named Bohemia after the Alpine Boii Tribe living there. The Czechs migrated from the Vistula River to central Europe. According to legend, they were guided by Čechus or Čech, their chieftain.

623 Frankish merchant Samo organized the Slavic tribes into a kingdom centered in Bohemia.

813–33 At the end of the eighth century, there were two princedoms on the territory of Slovakia: Pribina's in Nitra, and Mojmir's in Western Slovakia and Southern Moravia. The princedoms united and laid the foundation of the Great Moravian Empire.

862–94 Cyril and Methodius brought Christianity to Moravia. Part of their missionary work included creation of a Slav alphabet ensuring literary culture for these people. Great Moravia began to flourish under Prince Svatopluk.

907–929 The Magyars invaded Slovakia, ending the period of the Great Moravian Empire. The Slovak and Czech lands (Bohemia and Moravia) began periods of domination by different political forces. Duke Wenceslaus was murdered by his brother and became the patron saint of Bohemia.

965 The Jewish merchant Abraham Ben Jacob wrote the first description of the city of Prague, "built of stone and limestone," and termed it the "largest trading city in those lands."

1100–1400 The Holy Roman Empire invited German merchants, artisans, and miners to settle in Bohemia and Slovakia. From A.D. 500 to 1620, there were wars with German and Magyar invaders. Prince Vladislav II became King Vladislav I in 1158. He directed the building of Judith Bridge, the first stone bridge across the River Vltava.

1346–78 Charles IV reigned and Prague experienced its most glittering Golden Age, becoming the largest city in central Europe. Charles University, the first university in central Europe, was founded. The foundation for the famous Charles Bridge, replacing the Judith Bridge, was laid. Completed in 1399, the bridge is still standing today.

1415–36 Jan Hus, Bohemian religious reformer, was burned at the stake. The Hussite Wars and the First Defenestration of Prague were touched off by Hus' death, and rebellious Hussites, led by Jan Žižka, initiated decades of religious and ethnic warfare when several councillors were thrown from the window of the New Town Hall in Prague. Many German Catholics fled Bohemia.

1576–1741 Emperor Rudolph II's reign gave Prague a second Golden Age. Important European artists and scientists worked for the king. Protestant groups joined the Lutherans and drew up the *Confessio Bohemia,* officially the *Letter of Majesty of Rudolph II.* The Second Defenestration of Prague precipitated the Bohemian War, which later developed into the Thirty Years' War. In accordance with old Bohemian custom, two of the emperor's men and their secretary were thrown from a Council room window at Hradčany (Prague Castle), May 23, 1618, due to supposed violations of religious issues cited in the *Letter of Majesty.* On November 8, 1620, the Czechs were defeated by the Hapsburgs in the battle of White Mountain. The Czech crown lands were no longer independent, and approximately 36,000 families fled into exile.

Joachim Gans came with explorers in **1585** to Roanoke, North Carolina. Augustine Hermann was the first documented Czech settler in America in **1620**. He was a surveyor and draftsman, planter, fur trader, land developer, and successful merchant. Eventually, he became a diplomat.

In **1740,** Maria Theresa became the Hapsburg empress. Under her more liberal regime, Catholic control of education lessened and Czech culture began to revive. A year later in **1741**, groups of Moravian Brethren began to arrive in America, settling in Pennsylvania, North Carolina, and Georgia.

1848–1911 Revolts broke out in many European capitals, including Prague and Vienna. The Hapsburgs of Austria gained greater control with the Austrian lords holding the most valuable land. Czech peasant families lived on small plots. Big cities like New York, Chicago, and St. Louis attracted Czech craftsmen during the decades after the **1850s**. Others working in the cigar industry lived in New York City tenements under deplorable conditions.

The first documented Czech lawyer in the United States was Joseph Sosel, who was smuggled out of Bohemia when he opposed the established government. He settled in Cedar Rapids in the **1850s.**

In the next twenty years, rural areas of Texas and the Midwest attracted those seeking land ownership. A second wave of Czechs acquired land and settled in rural Nebraska and Kansas. From the Civil War era to **1911**, Czech peasants paid redemption fees, sold possessions, and came to America for cheap land.

The lure of the California gold rush mixed with failure of potato crops, floods, and droughts brought waves of Czech immigrants to America. Approximately 326 Czech newspapers flourished in America. The first Czech bank was established in Chicago in **1866.** A constant flow of Czechs settled in

Illinois, Iowa, Minnesota, Nebraska, Ohio, Wisconsin, and Texas.

1914–18 Czechs and Slovaks living abroad joined Czechs and Slovaks and other national groups of Austria-Hungary in their campaign for an independent state, leading to the new Republic of Czechoslovakia.

1918–1935 October 28, **1918**, the Bill of Rights the Republic of Czechoslovakia was signed in the historic town hall of Philadelphia, Pennsylvania, site of the signing of the United States Declaration of Independence. Tomáš G. Masaryk was elected the first president of Czechoslovakia. One of U.S. President Woodrow Wilson's Fourteen Points called for the self-determination of minorities in central Europe based on ethnic and language considerations. This doctrine and the defeat of Germany in World War I made possible the founding of a free Czechoslovakia. In **1918**, the Allies created the Czecho-Slovak Republic.

The nation was troubled from the start. Slovakia was more of a province than an equal partner. Many Czechs during the years of **1920** to **1933** immigrated to the United States. Cedar Rapids, Iowa, became noted for having the largest city population of Czechs per capita, with over one-fourth of the residents being of Czech descent.

On February 17, **1933**, Anton Cermak, the Bohemian-born politician who was Mayor of Chicago and master builder of the city's Democratic Party at the time, took an assassin's bullet intended for President Franklin D. Roosevelt. At the time of the shooting, Cermak uttered his famous line, "I am glad it was me instead of you." Cermak died within the month.

Adolph Hitler rose to power in Germany in **1933**, and called for the 3.5 million ethnic Germans living in the Sudeten district of Czechoslovakia to have autonomy. The Republic's position was precarious because of Nazi Germany's claims and invasion on the territories.

1935–1939 Eduard Beneš was elected the second president of Czechoslovakia. During World War II, his government was in exile in London, England. Neville Chamberlain, Prime Minister of Great Britain, in an agreement with France, gave in to Hitler's territorial demands for the Sudetenland. Hungary seized the Magyar area of Southern Slovakia and Poland took the city of Teschen. The Germans helped create a puppet republic in Slovakia and turned Bohemia and Moravia into a protectorate. Hungary absorbed Ruthenia.

1945 The provisional government of Beneš returned to Prague at the end of the war. Ruthenia was conceded to the Ukraine due to language and ethnic similarities of the people. Slovakia was granted autonomy within the Republic, and expulsion of the Germans began.

1946 In a May election, the Communists received thirty-eight percent of the vote, more than any other political party in Czechoslovakia. The February Communist coup d'etat in **1948**, when Soviet troops invaded, enabled the Communists to take control of Czechoslovakia's government, and a new constitution was drafted. Jan Masaryk, son of Tomáš Masaryk, plunged to his death from a palace window in Prague. It is still not known if his death was a murder or suicide, but it awakened America to the dangers of expanding Communism. President Beneš resigned. Klement Gottwald, Communist party leader, became president. Czechoslovakia was renamed a People's Democratic Republic. The government began collectivization of farm land and businesses.

1968 Alexander Dubček, a Slovak, became general secretary of the Czechoslovak Communist Party, lifting censorship and giving more freedom of religion and of the press, promising increased independence for Slovakia. This brief period of liberalization was known as the Prague Spring. In August, troops from the Soviet Union, Bulgaria, East Germany, Hungary, and Poland again invaded Czechoslovakia to resist the humanization of socialism.

1975 Charter 77, a declaration to protest then-President Gustáv Husák's harsh policies, was advanced by an emerging organization demanding greater freedom and independence. Their leader and future president, playwright Václav Havel, was imprisoned along with other signers of the document.

1989–90 Czechoslovakia was one of the last central European countries to take advantage of new liberal possibilities created by Soviet President Mikhail Gorbachev. Mass demonstrations and a general strike in November and December, **1989**, led to the peaceful Velvet Revolution. The existing government resigned and a democratic multi-party system was introduced with the repeal of the Communist Party's right of control. Dissident playwright Václav Havel became president. The country's name was changed to Czech and Slovak Federal Republic. Vladimir Meciar became political party leader in Slovakia.

1992 In June elections, Václav Klaus won a majority in Bohemia and Moravia. On July 17, Slovakia declared independence. President Havel resigned from office. By December, division of Slovak and Czech lands was completed.

1993–2004 January 1, Czech and Slovak Republics became independent, sovereign states. Václav Havel was elected president of the Czech Republic and Michal Kováč was elected the first president of the Slovak Republic.

    Three years after the peaceful Velvet Revolution in Czechoslovakia formalized the failure of Communism, the Czechs and Slovaks went their independent ways as the Czech and Slovak Republics. With the overthrow of Communism, the market economy began to emerge slowly. A stock exchange was formed. The Ministry of Privatization initiated the transfer to private ownership and control of many businesses and industries. Tourism became economically important.

The Czech term for the Czech lands (Bohemia, Moravia, Czech Silesia) is *Česko*, and since 1993 has been preferred by the Ministry of Foreign Affairs. Václav Klaus became second President of Czech Republic in **2003**.

2011–2012 On December 18, **2011**, the death of the first (post-Communist) president of the Czech Republic, Václav Havel, always a champion of human rights, is grieved. His life bespoke his moral platform and, until his death, he made an enormous impact on the world. Havel believed the Czechoslovak First Republic (1918–1938) was an era of enduring moral importance because Czechs and Slovaks demonstrated the ability to create and sustain a Republic that upheld civil liberties and social reform.

Like the Republic's first president, T.G. Masaryk, Havel encouraged his fellow citizens to persevere in the difficult task of maintaining and strengthening individual liberty with the politics of democracy.

A memorial plaque in Prague marks the place where Czechoslovakia's Velvet Revolution began with the massive public demonstration on November 17, 1989. Citizen protests grew until more than a half million people assembled in Letná Park in Prague on November 25–26, followed by a general strike that crippled the nation.

Václav Havel helped lead the November 1989 protest movement and was elected the first president of the post-Communist nation. The memorial plaque reads:

When—if not now? *(Kdy—Když Ne Teď?)*

Who—if not us?   *(Kdé—Když Ne My?)*

The Czech Republic

This landlocked Republic is bordered by Austria, Germany, Poland, and Slovakia. There are no seascapes and no deserts. Bohemia is in the west, with rolling plains, and Moravia is in the east, with forests and woodlands.

Bohemia is a 500-mile-high plateau, surrounded by low mountains that ring a basin drained by the Labe (upper Elbe River) and its tributary, the Vltava (Moldau). Moravia, mostly lowlands, is drained by the Morava River, and has few hills, including the White Carpathians. The area of the Czech Republic is 78,864 square kilometers. Its population numbers 10.5 million, and the capital is Prague. This is a parliamentary democracy, with a government headed by fifteen members, including a head of state, prime minister, and foreign minister.

The currency is the Czech crown. The economy is stable and prospering, one of the most prosperous of post-Communist countries. *Česko,* the official and preferred term for Czech Republic, has not been affected by the Eurozone crisis as much as other central European states. Major industries include road vehicles, machinery and electrical equipment, and industrial and office machinery and equipment.

The Czech company Mitas opened its first tire factory in the United States in Charles City, Iowa, in April, 2012. This is the largest Czech investment in the U.S., amounting to some $52 million USD. The plant's full capacity will be 13,500 metric tons of tires a year.

Regarding international relations, the Republic is part of Visegrad Group (V4), along with Slovakia, Hungary, and Poland. Czech Republic belongs to the United Nations, joined NATO in 1999 and the European Union in 2004, and plays an active role in international peace-keeping operations.

Tourism booms in *Česko,* one of the major tourist destinations in Europe. Prague is closer to London than Rome. Prague is the same longitude as Berlin. Go to Prague, but don't stop there! There is no other country in the world with more sights on the UNESCO World Heritage List, with twelve sites, two intangible heritage traditions, and one geopark. All are amazing! In addition to World Heritage sites, the Czech Republic boasts classic castles, and there is folk life and art, and spas. You may take the railways and enjoy public transportation in cities.

Prague: Eternal City, The Golden City, City of Seven Hills

Prague is as endearing as its descriptions, a city that has truly lived through the centuries. "Going from—toward" embodies the history of this city; the destination of those of us who travel there to experience its charms. Before recorded history, Prague's position as the crossroads of Europe made it greatly influential for trade and coveted for hundreds of years by invading forces. The Golden City enjoyed a golden age, especially during the reign of Charles IV, aided by Italian architects. Under his leadership, Prague grew in magnificence and was larger than Paris or London. The City of Seven Hills, Prague is also a city of the unexpected. Despite the fact that its position in central Europe has placed it in the middle of European conflicts, few cities anywhere can offer more than 600 years of architecture and history so untouched by natural disaster or war. Prague delights with lovely views, and its skyline is one of the most beautiful in Europe. Great castles and ornate spires rise gracefully above cobblestone streets, historic parks, cultural centers, indoor and outdoor restaurants, pubs, and cafés.

Prague originally developed as four separate, self-governing towns and a walled ghetto. Five spectacular areas are: Staré Mêsto (Old Town), Mála Strana (Little Quarter), Nové Mêsto (New Town), Hradčany (where Prague Castle is located), and Josefov (Jewish Quarter).

The medieval hub of the city is Staré Mêsto (Old Town), the heart of Prague. Its central Old Town Square is the center of Romanesque Prague. Through here is the road that connected with the ancient east-west trade route. This square is alive with shoppers, shops and booths alike, and delightful restaurants that serve inside and out. Old Town sites include unforgettable museums and galleries, churches, historic streets and squares, monuments and buildings, theaters, and a palace. Along Charles Street, among the many decorated homes on this ancient street, is an Art Nouveau depiction of Princess Libuse, who, according to Slav legend, founded the Premyslids, a family that ruled Prague from A.D. 900 until 1306.

Charles Street merges into the spectacular Charles Bridge, the Bridge of Saints, which features thirty sculpted saints, spanning some fifteen centuries. This bridge is easily the most popular historical monument, and it links Old Town to Little Quarter (Mála Strana).

Little Quarter, on the west bank of the River Vltava, is the second town of Prague. It was founded in 1257 to unify scattered Romanesque settlements that had grown up in the shadow of Prague Castle. Little Quarter climbs the slopes that lead uphill to the Castle complex.

New Town (Nové Mêsto) was established and carefully planned in 1348 by Charles IV to create more market space: Hay Market, Cattle Market, and Horse

Market (Wenceslaus Square). Twice as large as Old Town and adjacent to it, New Town was also created to make room for the city's booming economy and its increasing numbers of craftsmen, from blacksmiths and wheelwrights to brewers. New Town is imposing and heralds the power and influence it held in medieval times. Wenceslaus Square, about 750 metres in length and sixty metres wide, is a spectacular boulevard, bustling with shoppers, making it a contemporary marketplace probably much like it was as a horse market at its inception. Here is a spectacular twentieth-century statue of St. Wenceslaus on horseback. Just behind the statue of St. Wenceslaus is the National Museum with its monumental staircase.

The State Opera is in New Town, as is the National Theater. The idea for building a Czech National Theater was rejected by the country's ruling Austrians following the Thirty Years' War. Czech national pride began to be restored as Austrian rule relaxed, so the Czechs themselves purchased the land and built this theatre in 1881. Only two months after its completion, the theatre burned down. A testimony to Czech resolve to promote their own culture is that it was rebuilt and reopened just two years later with gilded stucco, crystal chandeliers, red plush seats, and curtains. The theatre was meticulously refurbished in the 1980s.

The history of Prague begins with the Prague Castle and Hradčany. Founded in the ninth century, it is a commanding center high above the Vltava. St. Vitus Cathedral, on its hilltop perch in the castle complex, is the most distinctive landmark in Prague; here all former Czech presidents have resided. In the middle ages, two Jewish communities, one from the West and the other from the Byzantine Empire, merged and were confined to an enclosed city. The Jews who lived there suffered from oppressive laws. Discrimination was relaxed in 1784 by Joseph II and the Jewish Quarter was named Josefov after him. Significant and memorable structures are the Jewish Town Hall, a number of synagogues, and the Old Jewish Cemetery, which was founded in the first half of the fifteenth century. Its oldest tombstone dates back to 1439.

As Prague continues "Going from—toward," few cities in Europe approach its appeal in terms of sights and historical and cultural experiences. Here Gothic, Baroque, Romanesque, and Art Nouveau complement one another. Prague offers a concentrated history blended with legends unsurpassed in romance and intrigue. Its beauty, as its name, has endured.

The Charles Bridge

The earliest bridges to connect the Old Town (Staré Mêsto) and the Lesser Quarter (Mála Strana) were wooden. The first stone bridge across the Vltava was built by King Vladislav I and named Judith Bridge in honor of his wife, Judith of Thuringia. Built between 1158 and 1172, the Judith Bridge collapsed under one of the Vltava's frequent floods in 1342. Charles IV commissioned a young architect, Peter Parler, to engineer the construction of a new stone bridge, however, the bridge was not completed until 1399. It was a forty-seven-year project.

For 400 years it was known as the Prague Bridge, or Stone Bridge. When this was the only bridge transversing the river, there was no need to specify the bridge by name. Other bridges had not been built when Charles IV embarked on his mid-fourteenth-century program of civic improvements. Finally, in 1870, other bridges had been erected and this impressive example of medieval engineering was named for its patron. The massive towers at each end, like the bridge itself, were designed for defense. With its width of thirty-three feet, this bridge could accommodate four carriages abreast. Its 1,706-foot span rests on sixteen arches. Today the Charles Bridge is the most familiar monument in Prague. It entertains steady streams of sightseers, souvenir seekers and sellers, and would-be statesmen, and is a popular spot to just "hang out."

For a long period of time, the bridge itself, with its majestic proportions and fine stonework, was the real work of art. Apart from a crucifix, there was no sculptural ornamentation until the end of the seventeenth century. Then, in 1693, on the 300th anniversary of the death of St. John of Nepomuk, the idea of Charles Bridge as a perfect setting for a statue of the saint was conceived. Other statues soon followed, with commemorations by religious institutions, faculties, private donors, and important officials. Some statues are a curious combination of saints that do not share a common theme or chronological base. Over the next 250 years, the number of individual statues reached thirty, plus the pillar of Roland (*Bruncvík* in Czech), legendary hero of the *Song of Roland,* which rests on a bridge pier as patron of the bridge. Nearly all of the sculptures on the Charles Bridge Avenue of Saints are of Bohemian sandstone, and because of deterioration due to atmospheric pollution, they are gradually being replaced by copies. The originals are held at the Lapidarium, the National Museum's repository of historic stone relics from the eleventh to nineteenth centuries. The Lapidarium also preserves the statue of St. Ignatius of Loyola, which, before it was washed away during a flood, stood at the position now occupied by Saints Cyril and Methodius.

Joan Liffring-Zug Bourret photos

The Charles Bridge   Český Krumlov

Český Krumlov

The special rhythm reveals a living gallery of picturesque and elegant Renaissance and Baroque-era structures housing homes, cafés, pubs, restaurants, galleries, businesses, and shops. Beautifully situated on the winding upper Vltava River, Český Krumlov is a uniquely-complete medieval townscape, with arch-covered footpaths and lanes of cobblestone winding up and down steep and narrow corridors. This jewel of a town represents another era in depth and breadth. The special rhythm of this southern Bohemia district town, about 105 miles south of Prague, is that of a town that has been bustling since medieval times.

Český Krumlov was first mentioned in writing in a 1253 document of the Austrian and Styrian Duke Otakar. "Český," meaning Czech, was added when the town was the seat of Vitek of Krumlov, a member of the Vitkovitz family. The Lords of Krumlov died out in 1302, and their estate was inherited by distant relatives, the Rozmberks. Henry from Rozmberk, the first Rozmberk, and his son Peter helped Český Krumlov attain town status more than 600 years ago, a feat difficult to attain. Town privileges entailed establishment of churches and monasteries. Handicrafts and trade were encouraged. The Rozmberks turned Český Krumlov into the center of their domain.

—13

Český Krumlov is split into two parts: there is the Inner Town and there is Latrán, which houses the castle. Few cars are allowed. Aside from the mansion tower and the castle building, the most dominant structure is the impressive late Gothic Church of St. Vitus. Its graceful, slender tower is visible from every point in the town. From the tower, there is a spectacular view of both Inner Town and the castle across the river. St. Vitus Church arose on the site of a small early four-teenth-century church, and was consecrated in 1439. The Town Hall (Radnice), located on the main square, boasts Gothic arcades and has an exceptionally beau-tiful Renaissance vault inside. Numerous houses with Renaissance facades line the narrow streets, and historic scenes and emblems are everywhere.

The Český Krumlov plague column is a point of fascination. Such columns form statuary in the squares of innumerable cities, towns, and villages in the Czech Republic. They were erected as thanksgiving by the living who were spared during the Black Death, which devastated Europe in the mid-1300s.

In 1374, the original town had only ninety-six houses. Town privileges were expanded and, in 1494, the Rozmberk brothers granted the so-called "royal right" to Český Krumlov, its suburbs, and villages. This designation conferred permission to freely leave property to any person, establishment of places where legal disputes and cases could be heard, and an obligation to keep the streets clean. Its uniqueness caused it to be declared a protected urban reservation in 1963. Český Krumlov's importance as an exceptional historical monument was emphasized again in 1992, when the town was entered in the UNESCO World Heritage Sites a register of monuments of world significance, "deserving extraor-dinary care, attention, and support."

Czech Republic UNESCO World Heritage Sites

Small wonder that tourism thrives in the Czech Republic. No other country has more sights and sites.

They include: Český Krumlov; Holašovice; Kroměříž; Kutná Hora; The Lednice-Vavltice area; Litomyšl; Prague; The Holy Trinity Column; Telč; Trebic-Basilica of St. Procope and Jewish Town; The Villa Tugendhat; The Pilgrimage Church of St. John of Nepomuk at Zelená Hora; Slovácko Verbuňk (Dance of Recruits) in Southeast Moravia; the Shrovetide processions in Hlinecko; and The Holy Trinity Column in Olomouc. Bohemian Paradise, a tourist destination in North Bohemia for nearly two centuries, became the first nature preserve in the Czech Republic in 1955. This area has a grand and dra-matic appearance with sandstone rock formations jutting out of its forests. About half of Bohemian Paradise has geopark status.

Charles University

When did Columbus discover America? A fact all school children know is that the date is 1492. At Charles University, founded in 1348, more than 140 years before America was discovered, there was a school where people were learning to be doctors, lawyers, architects, teachers, pharmacists, and many other occupations. This illustrates what "ancient" means in terms of cultures and countries. And those doctors, lawyers, and architects brought those skills with them when they settled in North America.

The oldest university in central Europe, Charles University is named in honor of Charles IV (then ruler of Bohemia). Today it is still a leading university—one of the world's best.

Hundreds of years are translated into hundreds of years of political conflicts (from the Thirty Years' War through Communist rule). At one point it was split into two universities: Czech and German. Charles University was home to world-reknown scholars and writers, such as Albert Einstein and Franz Kafka. Tomáš Garrigue Masryk, and Edvard Beneš, the first and second presidents of Czechoslovakia, were graduates.

Academic freedom, of course, has been disrupted over the years. In the 1980s, normalization began to occur. Students organized activities and peaceful demonstrations. Students and faculty played a large role in initiating the Velvet Revolution in 1989. Václav Havel was recruited from the independent academic community and appointed president of the Republic in 1989.

Museums in Prague

In the Eternal City of Prague, museums abound. Museums honor artists and writers, scientists, puppets, and religious and political viewpoints. The Mucha Museum, for example, is dedicated to the life and work of world-acclaimed Czech Art Nouveau artist Alphonse Mucha. Museums include:

Czech Republic Museum
   of Decorative Art
National Gallery
Josef Sudek Gallery (photography)
Antonín Dvořák Museum
Bertramka Mozart Museum
Franz Kafka Museum
Mucha Museum
Bedrich Smetana Museum

Museum of Communism
National Museum
Náprstek (Museum of Asian,
   African, and American Cultures)
National Technical Museum
Museum of the Prague Bambino
   (Infant of Prague)
Wax Museum
Puppet Museum

The Art of Living

Music, dance, objects of beauty, literature, and the mastering of crafts or skills—all are a part of "The Art of Living." These arts abound in the lives of Americans of Czech heritage. There is a Czech folk custom testifying to the importance of the arts in the hearts and minds of the Czech people. The custom says that a baby, when first interested in exploring objects around him, was offered a coin and a violin. If he chose the violin, he would become a musician and if he chose the coin, it was predicted that he would become a thief.

Before the Czech and Slovak families began immigrating to the United States in the early 1850s, they lived in a state of semi-serfdom in Bohemia. For more than 200 years before the 1850s, Austrian lords owned the most valuable land while the Czechs held small pieces of undesirable land. In those days music was a profession that enabled them to rise above their circumstances.

Accomplishments in the arts allowed one to accomplish something monetarily and to become someone. Without an art, a person might never hope to attain anything beyond the simple peasant life. Further, even if an accomplished artist did not make a living from one of the arts, the mastering of the art would set the artist apart from another tradesman or craftsman or farmer who had not mastered an art. To perform a task, the lords would hire the person who had a local reputation as an artist instead of hiring someone with fewer accomplishments. Art was much more than an injection of beauty and delight into the artist's world. It was an element of survival. The Czech people knew that skill in art could ensure success for future generations.

The Czech people are an ancient people, descendants of Slavic tribes first shown in the records in the fifth century. Theirs has been a history of struggling to preserve their heritage because it has been also a history of struggling against invasions of foreigners—outsiders who wanted Czech land and natural resources. The culmination of their struggle against invasions came with the Czech defeat by the Hapsburgs in the Battle of White Mountain, outside of Prague, in 1620. This battle ended the Czech crown lands' independence as a nation and, as a result, some 36,000 families eventually went into exile, choosing anywhere, including America, over the semi-serfdom rule of the Hapsburgs.

The first Czechs came to America in 1633. Many of these immigrants were farmers and were poor. Others had uncommon skills derived from a rich and ancient culture. For example, the first university in central Europe was established in Prague 100 years before Columbus discovered America. Czechs brought with them to America the first lawyer to settle west of the Mississippi, Joseph Sosel. A young lawyer who had taken part in a Prague uprising, he escaped from the Czech lands by being rolled across the border in a barrel. In

Cedar Rapids, Iowa, he learned English and taught others, and the new Czech community quickly stabilized. Sosel's daughters, Josephine and Mary, were principals of Cedar Rapids grade schools in the early 1900s.

The soul of a Czech has always found a voice in his music. In Bedřich Smetana, Czech music became an outlet for national feeling as well as the deeper emotions of the heart of the people—love of country, enjoyment of its beauties. "The Bartered Bride," an opera first produced in Prague in 1866, is still popular today in America. Another Czech, Antonín Dvořák, was inspired to complete his "New World Symphony" while living in Spillville, Iowa. This is a beautiful little Czech village on the banks of the Turkey River with a mill and the large St. Wenceslaus Catholic church built from fieldstone.

Czech immigrants were inclined to be clannish. They lived near Czech tradesmen, Czech banks, Czech theatres, and Czech stores. Fraternal organizations and clubs have long been important to Czechs. Through these groups, the heritage of the Czech people in America has been nurtured over the past 130 years. Many organized quilting and sewing groups still meet weekly and help ensure the continuation of traditional arts.

Some Czech and Slovak women retain the old country dracky, or feather stripping party, if only in a modified form. Geese are not easily come by these days! Feather stripping involves the sorting of goose feathers, separating the fine down from the quills. At Czech festivals, Marge Stone has demonstrated the making of pirkas, or feather basters, using only the seven or eight rounded feathers from the bottom of each wing. A pirka is just another kitchen tool, but it exemplifies an ethnic custom of charm and importance.

Czechs have always painted and decorated ornate eggs during the Easter season. As a child, Cedar Rapids, Iowa, artist Marj Nejdl "thought that everybody spent hours and hours decorating eggs at this season." Her work includes batik, or wax resist decorating, and handpainted and pen and ink designs and scenes. Physical fitness is also an art to the Czech people, and many Czechs credit the Sokol movement with making the most vital contribution toward fostering Czech heritage while also being a school for American democracy. The Czech people left behind them a land which knew a grand history and culture. Throughout generations of war and oppression in Europe, they maintained their heritage and brought that heritage, their music, arts, and customs to their new countries. Throughout North America, this heritage is being kept alive to reinvigorate today and to give confidence for tomorrow.

Czechs in the United States

According to the 2011 U.S. Census estimate, 1,508,360 Americans claim full or partial Czech descent, and 296,881 additional persons listed their ancestry as Czechoslovak. The first significant wave of Czech immigration to America occurred during the first half of the eighteenth century, when followers of religious reformer and martyr Jan Hus fled the difficult religious and political situation of his home country. The immigrants called themselves the Moravian Brethren. Many more Czechs immigrated to America during the nineteenth century, most settling in the Midwest to farm. As the twentieth century arrived, most new Czech immigrants were Catholic, unlike previous waves of immigration. In 1910, the Czech population reached 349,000. In 1970, the U.S. Bureau of the Census reported 800,000 Czechs living in America. However, this number did not count for Czechs who had been living in America for many generations. The top five states with Czech-American populations include: Texas (155,855), Illinois (123,708), Wisconsin (97,220), Minnesota (85,056), and Nebraska (83,462). The states with the highest percentages of Czech Americans among their populations include: Nebraska (5.5%), South Dakota (2.3%), North Dakota (2.2%), Wisconsin (2.1%), and Iowa (2.1%).

In a compilation of Texas settlements/towns by Cindy Harvey Neal entitled *Guide to the Czech Communities in Texas,* some 100 settlements in Texas have Czech names. About half of these settlements/towns still exist. These sites are noteworthy because of the early date they were established or because they are sites for historical events, churches, lodges, or buildings. You may want to peruse this site: www.czechheritage.org/communities.html for this extensive list.

Famous Czech Americans

There are many notable Americans of Czech descent. Madeleine Albright, former U.S. Secretary of State, was born in Prague. George W. Bush, the forty-third president of the United States, is of Czech ancestry on his mother's side. Anton Cermak, former mayor of Chicago, is credited with saving Franklin D. Roosevelt's life when he died after taking a bullet intended for the president. Jerome Kern, twentieth century American theatre composer, is also of Czech descent. Actress Sissy Spacek is of Czech descent on her father's side. Raymond Kroc joined McDonald's in 1954 and built it into the most successful fast food restaurant in the word. In the world of science, Frank Malina, aeronautical engineer and designer of the first U.S. rocket to break the fifty-mile altitude mark, and Eugene Cernan, the last astronaut of Apollo to leave his footprints on the moon, have Czech heritage.

The Moravians Came Early

This Ephraim Moravian Church (Unity of Brethren), above, in Door County, Wisconsin, is a part of a faith heritage of more than 500 years, arguably the first Protestant church. This historic church has its roots in ancient Bohemia and Moravia. Jan Hus wanted to return to several principles of the church that were upheld in the territories of Bohemia and Moravia when they were Eastern Orthodox. His protest movement led to a lengthy trial in which he was declared a heretic and, subsequently, burned at the stake. As with many faiths, the Moravian Church suffered persecution.

On the other hand, the Moravian Church succeeded remarkably. The church provided the people of Bohemia and Moravia with a Bible in their own language. One of its most famous churchmen was the last bishop of the Moravian Church in Moravia, Jan Ámos Komenský (John Comenius, 1592–1670), who today is world famous for his progressive views on universal education. Zeal for evangelism was brought to England by the Moravian Brethren, and by the church ministers to people all over the world. They strongly influenced John and Charles Wesley, who founded the Methodist Church.

The first Moravians came to America in 1735–40. They founded the town of Bethlehem, Pennsylvania, in 1741, organizing their church there in 1744. Their symphony orchestra was the first in America. In 1766, they founded Salem (from *shalom,* the Hebrew word for peace), New Jersey. North Carolina was another stronghold of this faith in America. At the time of the Declaration of Independence in 1776, more than 2,000 Moravians lived in the Colonies. The first Moravian Church members to arrive in America were deeply religious, but were not austere. They dressed in bright attire and enjoyed good food, good music, and good fabrics!

Woodrow Wilson Monument Dedication

We owe more than one monument to the United States.

—Václav Havel

Four days of celebration in Prague in October, 2011, accompanied the unveiling and dedication of a monument honoring Woodrow Wilson, the twenty-eighth President of the United States. The monument commemorated a century of friendship between the United States and the Czech Republic. Former Czech President Václav Havel and former U.S. Secretary of State Madeleine K. Albright participated in the events and served as honorary co-chairpersons at the gala award dinner.

Built originally in 1928 to honor Wilson's support for Czechoslovakian independence, the monument was destroyed in 1941 during Nazi occupation. Seventy years later, this monument has been re-built near the original site outside of Prague's main train station, which bears Wilson's name.

"Many credit Czech independence to the Velvet Revolution of 1989, but the movement for freedom in my country truly began in the early twentieth century, as Tomáš Masaryk fought for independence from Austria-Hungary," said Havel. "Encouraged and informed by President Wilson and succeeding U.S. presidents, the Czech spirit survived through decades of Nazi and Communist rule to re-emerge in the Velvet Revolution and create what is now a free and independent Czech Republic," Havel continued. He spoke during ceremonies and also placed a bouquet at the foot of the monument.

"The story of the Wilson Monument, its destruction and resurrection, is the story of a friendship between two nations that has lasted for nearly 100 years," said Fred Malek, chairman of the American Friends of the Czech Republic (AFoCR) and former adviser to four U.S. presidents.

Gail Naughton, President/CEO National Czech & Slovak Museum & Library said, "Through the years I have continued to be inspired by the poignant Czech and Slovak stories of freedom and identity, family and community, human rights, and dignity that are shared with us almost daily at the NCSML...It is clear that these same values underpinned the enduring values for a peace settlement shared by Woodrow Wilson and T.G. Masaryk."

"I am thrilled to join President Havel, the American Friends of the Czech Republic, and the people of Prague in celebrating and honoring President Wilson's contributions to a free and independent Czechoslovakia," said Madeleine Albright, who was born in Prague during the period of Czechoslovak independence between World Wars I and II. "The Czech Republic continues to be a strong ally of the United States and an example of freedom and democracy in central Europe," Albright noted.

Photos courtesy of the National Czech & Slovak Museum & Library

Gail Naughton, President/CEO of the National Czech & Slovak Museum & Library, is shown with her husband Dennis Naughton at the reception following the Wilson Monument Dedication in Prague.

Canadians of Czech Ethnicity

The pattern of Czech immigration to Canada is similar to that in the United States. The first wave, 1880s to 1914, was dominated mainly by economic necessity. People wanted to own land and find work. Before the 1880s, Czech immigrants to the New World settled primarily in the United States, mostly where land was available in Nebraska, Texas, Oklahoma, Iowa, Minnesota, and Illinois. The majority of the first Czech immigrants to Canada were farmers settling in prairie provinces like Esterhazy, in southeastern Saskatchewan, where Slovaks and Hungarians had already settled. New Czechs settled wherever land was available. Western Canada had plentiful, inexpensive land and many from the Czech lands were recruited with resettlement offers.

Prague, in Alberta, was settled initially by Czech Americans from the U.S. There were also Czech urban communities like those in Edmonton, settled in early 1900. Between the two world wars, Czech immigrants settled in Montreal and Toronto. The 1931 census records 30,000 Canadian Czech residents. Many Czech immigrants arriving in Canada from 1945–89 were political refugees fleeing the Communist regime. Most were white collar, clerical, lawyers, artisans, and students. Although skilled and educated, many worked wherever they could in order to enter Canada and stay there. This underemployment was disadvantageous, since many, particularly women, had fled without educational and professional certification needed to get better jobs. They had to quickly acquire language skills and work experience, with many assisted by Czech-owned Canadian businesses. An estimated 21,000 Czechs came as refugees between 1968 (the Prague Spring invasion by Soviet troops) and 1969. The government funded language classes and other programs for immigrants settling predominantly in urban areas. The 2006 census recorded 99,000 Canadians of full or partial Czech descent.

The Sokol (falcon) movement, emphasizing athletic and patriotic values, is well-established in Canada. Toronto enjoys a vibrant Czech community, with a Czech Language Meetup, where Czechs get together to practice fluency with the Czech language. Prague Restaurant is in the natural setting of Masaryktown Park in Toronto. This contemporary Euro-Canadian restaurant offers a wide range of Canadian and European dishes, including famous Czech-Slovak cuisine. A touch of eighteenth-century English history enhances the international ambience and spells home for those who yearn for a good Czech meal. There is a Canadian embassy in Prague (Czech Republic) and the Czech Republic has an embassy in Ottawa, a consulate general in Toronto, and two honorary consulates in Calgary and Winnipeg.

Traditions from Decades Past

Some of the age-old traditions observed, beginning with Svatý Mikuláš Day and Advent, are a part of preparing for Christmas Day. In ancient times, finding a good husband was of paramount importance to girls, and many pre-holiday games revolved around predictions of just whom a girl would marry. On December 4, St. Barbara's Day, a branch of a cherry tree (or other flowering tree) was broken off and placed in a pot of water in the kitchen; the twig usually burst into bloom at Christmas time, making a festive decoration. The bloom was also considered good luck, and if a girl of marrying age tended it to bloom exactly on Christmas Eve, she was supposed to find a good husband within the year. A further foretelling of the gift of a good husband was dropping melted lead into a pan of cold water; the shape the lead took as it cooled was a forecast of the future husband's occupation. If girls drew sticks from a pile of kindling wood, a long stick meant a tall husband, a thick stick meant a stout husband, and so on.

Many of the Christmas trees were decorated with handmade ornaments, some using walnut shells and pralines wrapped in colored papers with finely cut and curled edges. Another specialty is the use of eggshells decorated to look like strange fish or representations of the angel who accompanied Sv. Mikuláš. There are colored pinwheels resembling snowflakes and twinkling stars suspended by thread. Gilded walnuts and many varieties of bells are hung in clusters on bright ribbons. A small crèche is often placed at the base of the tree. A blessing is thought to be received if the children spent a night sleeping on a bedding of straw and hay placed near the tree. This custom allows them to take part in the poor and humble birth of the Christ Child. Traditionally there is caroling in the streets and homes and dancing and eating after the fasting period, which ends on Christmas Eve, with a special dinner. It is customary at this time for those who have quarreled during the year to forgive each other publicly. For this season, a large carp may be prepared in four different ways. Best cuts are coated with flour, dipped in egg, coated with bread crumbs, and fried. Lesser cuts are baked a la black with prunes and served with dumplings. A third preparation is a la blue (*na modro*). This is carp prepared with gelatin as rosol and served cold. The head and tail of the carp are wrapped in white cloth and boiled for a soup, usually with finely-cut carrots and other vegetables. Christmas Eve supper might include soup, pearl barley with mushrooms, carp, fruits, and decorated cookies. Carp is the traditional food, but other fish might be served. Dinner on Christmas day often includes giblet soup with noodles, roast goose with dumplings and sauerkraut, braided coffee cake, kolaches, fruits and nuts, and coffee.

St. Stephen's Day, December 26

The day after Christmas is a day for children to go from house to house caroling, and to receive candies, cookies, and other special seasonal treats.

January 1

On New Year's Day it is suggested that one eat pork for good luck and lentils for prosperity. If one eats fish, luck would swim away; if one eats poultry, luck would fly away.

Three Kings' Day, January 6

In some villages, residents write K † M † B on doorways to bring blessings to the building. Traditionally, three men dressed as the Three Kings would go caroling, and with a piece of chalk blessed by a priest, inscribe Kaspar, Melchior, and Balthazar above doorways to bring blessings on that home and family for the year.

St. Joseph's Day, March 19

Czechs think red every year on March 19. St. Joseph's Day is the Czech version of St. Patrick's Day, but there is little religious significance. Instead, it is a day to celebrate the Czech people by honoring the most common Czech name, Josef. In Czechoslovakia, St. Joseph's Day was always a communal day, an occasion for fun and gaiety. In Cedar Rapids' Czech Village, the taverns serve red beer, the bakeries sell red bread, and the village is decorated with red flowers.

Easter

A custom in both Čechy and Moravia at Easter was that of the boys weaving willow wands and "switching" the girls. This switching was accomplished for many reasons according to the locale. Sometimes girls were switched to get the devil or mischief out of them, or so they wouldn't be lazy. Switching also signified the casting off of winter's bleakness and dust. Decorated eggs were given to the tormentors, and virtually everyone, including the family cows and geese, were given eggs for luck in the coming year. When the eggs were eaten, the shells were spread on the fields and garden areas for luck for the growing season.

For Easter, a baked ham or roasted kid (young goat) is featured by many families. The sweet bread *(houska* or *vánočka)* that is baked for Christmas is the very same dough, round-shaped with raisins and almonds *(mazanec),* that is almost a must for Easter.

Worker's Day, May 1

A holiday celebrated by most European nations.

Mushroom Houby Days

In May each year is a celebration of spring and mushrooms. See page 27 for information about the importance of mushrooms from May to October.

Legend of the Frost

Gardeners watch their favorite signals to determine when to plant. A Czech legend warns not to plant before May 12, 13, or 14, because of the "three frozen kings" or "three frost saints." Pangrac (also Pangras) died May 12, A.D. 304. Servac (also Servais or Servitus) died on a May 13 and Bonifac (or Tarsus) died on a May 14. Then, on May 15, Sophia (Zofie) brought about a thaw with a kettle of boiling water. Sophia undoubtedly was brought into the legend because her feast day is May 15 and because she was known for her excellent cooking and baking. So, on May 15 or later, it's safe to plant.

When May temperatures threaten frost, the legend is especially recalled. In the New World, this legend applies to parts of Canada and northern United States. Elsewhere, gardens are planted in March or April, and in some southern areas the climate permits planting year-round. In Moravia, a five-foot figure representing the death of winter was drowned in a river on the first day of spring. The beginning of spring is heralded!

Saints Cyril and Methodius Days, July 5

Czechs celebrate the Monks Cyril and Methodius who brought Christianity to the Slavs.

Jan Hus Day, July 6

Celebrated in the Czech lands, but not in Slovakia which does not have Protestant heritage.

Independence Day, October 28

Czechs celebrate their independence after World War I.

Harvest Celebrations

There are two harvest celebrations in the Czech Republic: one held by the Catholic church as a consecration of the harvest *(Posvícení)* and one as the secular celebration *(Dožínky)*. Wreaths made of rye, field flowers, and ears of corn are placed on the heads of pretty girls. Later these wreaths are saved until the next harvest. A typical Czech feast includes: roast pig, roast goose, kolaches filled with prunes, sweet yellow cottage cheese, or poppy seed filling, beer, and prune liquor.

All Saints' Day

In the Czech Republic, All Saints' Day *(Dušičky)* is celebrated the day after All Souls' Day, usually early November. Similar to Memorial Day, it is a time for graves of loved ones to be decorated with flowers and lighted candles.

A Special Czech Myth

There is an old Czech myth about a king and his three daughters. The king decided to test his daughters to see which one loved him the most. He asked them what they would give him if they could choose from anything in the kingdom—what would be the most precious thing they would give him? The oldest daughter said she would give him all the gold in the world. The next daughter said she would give him all the silver in the world. The youngest daughter smiled and said she would give him salt. The king was outraged to think that his daughter loved him so little as to give him only a common kitchen spice. But the king tried to live without salt in his diet and quickly realized that salt was far more important than all the gold and silver in the world. It is customary to this day to welcome a visitor in a Czech home with a slice of rye bread sprinkled with salt.

—Mana Zlatohlavek, Cedar Rapids, Iowa

Moravian Folk Custom: Ride of the Kings

Processions, which played at being king, went around on Whitsunday to visit Czech, Moravian, and Silesian villages. This custom survives in only a few places, notably the Moravian village of Vlčnov. The King and his entourage pass through the entire village on horseback, stopping in front of each house. The crier passes either a positive or negative judgment on each dwelling's inhabitants. His proclamations are based upon whether the family may have broken the established rules of morality. The truth behind the procession is shrouded in the mystery of ancient times. For instance, why is the figure of the king dressed in women's clothing, clenching a rose between his teeth so he is unable to speak? Why are the horses veiled and decorated? There are a variety of legendary explanations, but the charm lies in the glimpse of a world that no longer exists.

According to legend, the crowned two-tailed lion has been the emblem of the Czech state since the mid-twelfth century.

Czech Out These Czech Festivals

Vítáme Vás (We Welcome You) is the theme for all!

Please accept spelling of kolač *(singular) and* kolače *(plural) any and all ways used. Liberties are taken with this pastry and its spelling!*

There is surely at least one such festival in or near your state where Czechs and their friends celebrate their culture with food, music, parades, royalty, contests, and fun. Among the many vibrant events, the following sites are home to an annual festival of two to three days' duration over the weekend.

Illinois: See page 45 for United Moravian Societies folklore celebration, Moravian Day in Chicago is celebrated each year in September.

Iowa: Houby Days (Mushroom Days) in Czech Village, Cedar Rapids. Always the weekend after Mother's Day in May, when houby generally abound, is the date of this three-day affair. Featuring "A Taste of Czech & Slovak" that kicks off the event, some thirty samples of foods are available, as well as beer. There are booths, a parade, competition for Miss Iowa Czech-Slovak Queen, houby to eat, and a houby competition. The National Czech & Slovak Museum & Library, taverns, restaurants, and shops feature favorite Czech items.

    Masopust (meatless) pre-Lenten celebration has been revived in recent years in the Czech Republic and the United States. To get one's fill of eating and amusement before Lent is the main goal of this carnival tradition. The event is held just prior to Ash Wednesday, which is one of the *masopust*/meatless days to be observed during Lent. This carnival event originated in the Middle Ages, and again today offers abundance and merriment. It is the Czech version of Mardi Gras, an occasion familiar to us in the United States.

Wild Mushroom Season
From May to October, gathering wild mushrooms from the woods is a popular and practical pastime in Central Europe. Both Czechs and Slovaks consider the many varieties of seasonal mushrooms as delicacies, whether cooked simply with scrambled eggs, or prepared in any number of original and traditional recipes.
Right: *Dressed as a morel mushroom, this man waves during the Houby Day parade in Cedar Rapids.* Russ De Hoedt photograph

In Protovin, Iowa, the Czech Heritage Partnership celebrates *Masopust* the weekend before Lent with a scrumptious Czech meal, served buffet style, Czech music and polka dancing, as well as skits and attendance by Czech youthful royal courts. Czechs from eastern Iowa often journey to the Protovin event by bus, and it is great time to enjoy during the bleakness of winter!

Kansas: Wilson, known as the Czech Capital of Kansas, was founded in 1865. Their festival is the last of July. The town has a few dozen limestone buildings built during the nineteenth and twentieth centuries.

Maryland: The Czech and Slovak Heritage Association of Maryland sponsors the annual Czech and Slovak Festival in Baltimore in October. Featured are folk dancers, displays, Czech and Slovak items, and food prepared by Bohemian caterers. Participants enjoy singing, dancing, beer, and Czech food. Sokol Baltimore began July 7, 1872 and has been in existence for 140 years.

Minnesota: Kolacky Days in Montgomery is celebrated in July. Started in 1929, this festival includes a Queen Pageant, home-baked kolacky contest, classic car show, a beer garden, and traditional Czech food. Other festivals are at New Prague and at St. Paul.

Missouri: Czech Festival, at the American Czech Education Center in St. Louis, is a one day event held in April. Everything from accordion music to imported Czech beer is offered, as well as delicious and authentic Czech food, deli selections, and pastries. The festival also includes a boutique and cooking demonstrations.

Nebraska: Wilber Czech Festival is always the first weekend in August. For more than fifty years, this Czech Capital of the U.S.A. has been a major festival attraction, hosting the Miss Czech-Slovak U.S. Pageant. This queen contest brings contestants who have been named queens in some ten state pageants. An Accordion Jam is featured. There is a parade for children as well as for grown-ups, and these parades attract hundreds of entries. Enjoy traditional music and dancing and bring a lawn chair to wile away the hours when you are not on your feet! Lots of Czechs celebrate in Nebraska. The following communities have special events: Clarkson; Lincoln; Butler County (David City); Prague; Panhandle (Lodgepole); Omaha; South Central (Hastings); and York. All have variations of fun, and Prague features the baking of the World's Largest Kolache.

Ohio: Český Den (Czech Day) is held in Taborville, twenty-five miles east of Cleveland. This is a Sunday event held in July and there is a gate fee. All proceeds go toward support of the following: Bohemian National Hall, home of Sokol Greater Cleveland on Broadway in Cleveland; Ceska Sin Sokol on Clark Avenue in Cleveland; and DTJ Pavillion in Taborville. Great food, music, events, door prizes, and raffles. The 2012 event was their eighty-ninth.

Oklahoma: Oklahoma Czech Festival is held the first Saturday in October in Yukon. Their promotional material reads, "Polka dancin' ... Dumplin eatin'... kolache makin'... and more." Sounds fun and a great way to get to know some Czechs.

South Dakota: Czech Days in Tabor are typically held the third Friday and Saturday in June. Thousands attend this event in a small community where Czech settlers arrived as early as 1869. The event offers *kolače*, the Beseda Dance, Polka Mass, Polka bands and dancing, a parade, and more!

Texas: Westfest, in the central Texas town of West, is a Czech/Polka Festival each Labor Day weekend. There is music, dancing, and a Kolache Fun Run. In Victoria, the Czech Heritage Festival in September begins with a mass in Czech and English. The festival offers traditional Czech food, a homemade beer and wine show, cultural demonstrations, games, and music. Other festival towns include Caldwell, East Bernard, Ennis, Hallettsville, Corpus Christi, and Houston.

Wisconsin: Cěský Den Czech Heritage Festival in Hillsboro, the Czech Capital of Wisconsin. A two-day event the first weekend in June. Featuring a queen pageant, Yuba/Hillsboro Czech Singers, antique tractor display, a parade both days, beer garden, and traditional foods!

May Pole   *Couple*   *Good Day*

Designs for folk art magnets and postcards by Marj Nejdl

Phillips, Wisconsin
Annual June Festival Celebrates Historic Roots
While Paying Tribute to the Sorrowful Memory of Lidice

When we cherish a bond with the past, we celebrate proudly the beautiful and glorious and also acknowledge that which prompts memories of regret and sorrow. In the small, northern Wisconsin community of Phillips, the Annual Phillips Czech-Slovak Festival events of gaiety are combined with commemoration of a horror played out in Czechoslovakia in World War II.

Phillips' Lidice Monument honors the people of Lidice, a village in the Czech Republic. The Lidice Monument invokes historical recollection of June 10, 1942, when Lidice was razed by Nazi Gestapo in an effort to punish the Czech Resistance for killing one of the Third Reich's own: Reinhard Heydrich, a sadist who supposedly was "the protector" of Czechoslovakia. Some 176 men were killed, while all women were sent to concentration camps. Boys age sixteen and under and all girls were sent away to be Germanized. The Gestapo even re-routed streams and rivers to eradicate any trace of Lidice, after burning the village and poisoning the land.

People world-wide raised money to build tributes to Lidice, to remember the former villagers, as well as other Czechs who were killed during Nazi occupation. Some Phillips residents had close ties to Lidice and built a temporary marker in 1943. The permanent Lidice Monument, the only such U.S. memorial designed and built by Czech immigrants, is on the National and State Registry of Historic Places, and was dedicated in 1944.

Another U.S. Lidice Monument is in Crest Hill, Illinois. A third monument is located in a small town re-named Lidice, near Rio de Janerio, Brazil. The fourth and largest monument to the village and its people is at the site of the original Lidice, Czech Republic.

Symbolism in the Memorial at Phillips

The large red stone pillar is symbolic of the United Nations and there are three rods to the left leaning into it. The three rods represent the Czechs, Moravians, and Slovaks leaning on the United Nations for assistance. The evergreen spray is symbolic of everlasting life hoped for the victims of Lidice and the rising sun behind the monument to the right is to portray the hope that Lidice and the Czech nation would rise again.

Photo courtesy Phillips Chamber of Commerce

Lidice Monument, Phillips, Wisconsin

IN MEMORY OF LIDICE
CZECHOSLOVAKIA
WHOSE CITIZENS
PERISHED BY NAZI
BRUTALITY
JUNE 10, 1942

LEST WE FORGET

TRUTH SHALL PREVAIL

Vicky Soliman photograph

*Crest Hill, Illinois, honors the memory of the people of Lidice, murdered by
the Nazi Gestapo in 1942.*

Czech Museum, Wilber, Nebraska

This small town is the Czech Capital of the U.S.A., and is located just thirty-five miles from Lincoln. The Museum features an outstanding collection of imported Czech dolls, beautiful Czech dishes, pictures, and replicas of early immigrant homes and businesses. The museum is open afternoons daily except holidays and also by appointment.

Prague Historical Museum and Annex Prague, Oklahoma

This museum in an attractive red building contains a collection of artifacts of early Prague and its Czech pioneers, in a community that began in 1891 when four Indian reservations were open for settlement. This building houses Prague Bohemian Hall and a general store area. This site is the centerpiece of the Prague Kolache Festival in Prague, the Kolache Capital of Oklahoma.

Bily Clock Museum & Antonín Dvořák Exhibit, Spillville, Iowa

One hundred years ago, in 1913, brothers Frank and Joseph Bily shared a hobby that became a passion. Iowa farmers and carpenters, their land was located between Ridgeway and Spillville. Frank and Joseph created intricate, hand-carved clocks that depicted art, culture, religion, and history. Most of their clocks have chimes and movable, wood-carved figures. A variety of woods were used, including walnut, maple, rosewood, butternut, oak, and white ash. The brothers never sold any of their clocks, but instead gave them to Spillville in 1946. These masterpieces are now in the Bily Clock Museum in Spillville. On the second floor is an exhibit in memory of Czech composer, Antonín Dvořák, who along with his family spent the summer of 1893 in the building.

Left: *The violin clock featuring Dvořák*

The National Czech & Slovak Museum & Library Cedar Rapids, Iowa

The National Czech & Slovak Museum & Library (NCSML) was founded by the Czech Fine Arts Foundation in 1978. The museum was dedicated in October, 1995, with a grand fanfare that included the United States President Bill Clinton, President Václav Havel of the Czech Republic, and President Michal Kováč of the Slovak Republic.

NCSML is the leading United States institution to preserve and interpret Czech and Slovak history and culture. It is in Cedar Rapids because twenty-five percent of area Cedar Rapidians claim Czech heritage. Generations of Czechs in the area support the mission of NCSML. For more than 142 years, a Czech School, one of the oldest and longest-running such schools in the United States, conducts a five-week session every summer. Czech language classes are held for adults as well.

The museum acquired accreditation with the American Alliance of Museums in 2008, a distinction received by only five percent of all museums in the United States.

A Monumental Move

During the flood of 2008 when the Cedar River waters surged out of its banks, the NCSML was positioned in what became the main channel of the river. Swamped with eight feet of water, NCSML sustained damage to the building along with exhibits, stored items, and some of its collection. Based on that flood, one of the most significant natural disasters in United States history, other museums would not loan items and NCSML could no longer insure its own collection or host exhibitions. Private donors would be reluctant to donate their treasures to the museum.

With the Museum building deemed structurally sound, NCSML leaders decided to stay in the Czech Village. In order to do so, it was decided to move the building. They raised twenty-five million dollars to move the museum and library building to higher ground. The museum is now raised to three feet above the 2008 high water line, repaired, and adjoins a 30,000 square foot addition, for a total size of 50,000 square feet. The original museum weighed 1,400 tons, roughly the equivalent of thirty-five full semi-trailers. Forty workers prepared for the move. Preparations included placing steel beams on forty dollies beneath the structure, starting in April 2011. The actual move of several days was conducted in mid-June. Spectators were welcome, souvenirs of the move were available, lip smacking koláče, and glasses of beer were raised in toasts in neighborhood pubs and eateries. The cost of the move was $713,000. Today the original red roof edifice has a permanent exhibition area and has doubled in size. A 5,500 square foot library housing 30,000 items is available to the public. Oral histories, genealogical services, and research are conducted. There is a multi-purpose public and educational program space. Three galleries offer permanent and temporary exhibitions, and there is a theatre for films, lectures, and other programs. Collections, original artwork, and artifacts are displayed. An outdoor amphitheater for heritage festivals and other programming is on site.

Moving the Museum to higher ground   *John Johnson photographs*

NCSML Mission and Collection
By Stefanie Kohn, NCSML Curator

The National Czech & Slovak Museum & Library collection includes more than 10,000 artifacts and is constantly growing. The museum's artifact holdings include a fabulous Czechoslovak car and motorcycle, an impressive collection of carved wooden furniture and figures, a significant holding of pins, ribbons, and paraphernalia related to Czech and Slovak American fraternal societies, groups of rare posters and buttons produced during political upheavals in twentieth century Czechoslovakia, a large collection of dolls dressed in ethnic folk costume, an outstanding collection of immigrant trunks and baskets, a brilliant assortment of glass, crystal, porcelain, and pottery, and an exceptional collection of Czech and Slovak textiles.

The textile collection includes complete *kroje* (folk costumes), household linens, beaded purses, leather goods, and other decorative accessories. All of these objects were produced or used by Czechs, Slovaks, or Americans of Czech or Slovak descent. Because many of these objects were brought over to the United States with their immigrant owners, their significance is reinforced. Immigrants generally were forced to select a very small set of their belongings to carry with them to their new lives and homes. Collection artifacts directly support the NCSML mission and programming which includes exhibits, educational curricula, public programs, school tours, and outreach presentations. Past exhibits have focused on the immigration experience of Czechs and Slovaks.

The National Czech & Slovak Museum & Library. At the far right of the Museum is the tiny Sleger immigrant home.

One popular exhibit was *Embellished Textiles: Absolutely Art,* consisting of more than 100 individual decorated textiles and fifteen *kroje.* Other original NCSML exhibits were *Liberation* that told the story of Czech and Slovak involvement in World War I, and *1968: Twelve Volatile Months that Changed the World.* These exhibitions drew upon the NCSML's collection of political and military items. Researchers make use of the NCSML holdings, including ethnographers who study the goddess motif in ancient European folk art. The goddess appears in many traditional Czech and Slovak embroidery patterns. Others look for patterns of dress and adornment that are common to all of Europe.

The collection supports humanities-related research, education, and programming, especially in the arts, history, world languages, and traditions that shaped our diverse cultural heritage. Themes and topics including art, history, ethics, and literature are addressed through the story and culture of the Czech and Slovak people worldwide. The preservation and interpretation of these collections is vital because the NCSML is the only major institution in the United States that actively collects, preserves, and interprets artifacts related to the history and culture of Czechs, Slovaks, and those of Czech and Slovak descent. This rich heritage is an important part of the overall American story and all people, regardless of ethnic background, can benefit from the stories we tell. Nearly half of the NCSML collection is made up of textiles. Czechs and Slovaks have a rich tradition of embellished textiles. Examples include everyday household linens such as towels, table cloths, and doilies. A splash cloth is a specific household linen that was hung behind a sink to protect the wall from water spatters. These splash cloths are embroidered with illustrated sayings that may be pithy, humorous, or sentimental: "If you don't like our house then go home and make yours better," and "She who over salts the meal must serve more beer." Other textiles include everyday clothing worn by immigrants on the journey to the United States as well as items worn in their new homes, and to high events such as weddings, funerals, festivals, and church. Many are heavily embellished with beads, appliqué, and embroidery. While the majority of the museum's holdings are women's costumes, it also owns several *kroje* for men and children. Many were brought over with immigrants and worn in the ethnic festivals and events in the United States. Others were purchased by private collectors for their beauty. Traditional *kroje* are no longer commonly worn or made in the Czech Republic and Slovakia. Both countries presently restrict the removal of this cultural property from their borders, making the holdings in the United States a rare resource. The NCSML continues to collect and preserve these stunning examples of art.

Before 1850, there were seventeen areas in Bohemia and over forty districts in Moravia where people wore folk costumes. In the borderland between Moravia and Slovakia, there were twenty-seven such districts at the beginning of the twentieth century. *Kroje* are historically significant. Shawls and kerchiefs show Gothic influence. Renaissance touches might be fine pleats and gathered lace, while bell-shaped skirts and oriental patterns borrowed from Turkish invaders depict Baroque touches. At first glance folk costumes appear generally as festive, colorful, and elaborate to the point of ostentation. However, depending on the district of origin and the purpose for which the costumes were created, all are different from one another. Some of the most beautiful costumes originated during periods of cruel oppression, when peasants suffered under serfdom and decorated *kroje* as one way to demonstrate personal individuality, self-expression, and taste. One's *kroj* was also a symbol of status and nationality. Differences in geographic location influenced differences in costume design and decoration.

The woman's cap is from Milotice, Moravia.
The shoes are from Domažlice.
Kroje *shown (on page 37) dates from mid-to-late 20th century.*

Women's kroje *are from Velká and Velicko, Moravia*

Man's kroj *is from Dolní Bojanovice, Moravia*

Scarf is from Domažlice, Bohemia

Photos courtesy of the National Czech & Slovak Museum & Library

NCSML Oral History Project

Recording Voices & Documenting Memories of Czech & Slovak Americans forms a fascinating presentation at the National Czech & Slovak Museum & Library, Cedar Rapids, Iowa. This oral history project, begun in 2009, preserves Czech and Slovak history and culture from 1948 to 1968 and beyond. Interviews and videotapes of individuals who escaped or left their homeland when the Communists seized power are featured, and how those events impacted their families and themselves give us remarkable stories.

This project, carried out by Rosie Johnston, NCSML oral historian, particularly focuses on Czechs and Slovaks in Chicago, Cleveland, New York City, the San Francisco Bay Area, and Washington, D.C. Visit the NCSML website: www.ncsml.org. Click on "oral histories" to learn more about the project, see snippets of interviews, and view photos and archival information.

Museum Guild

It is no secret: without volunteers, our Czech endeavors would not make it! Whether donations of money, time, travel; hosting visitors for events; preserving and demonstrating the decorative arts; maintaining traditional cooking; teaching and performing traditional music; needlework; or organizing pageants and staging festivals, volunteers make the difference. The Guild of NCSML has a mission that supports the activities, programs, and facilities. This mission is accomplished by providing unpaid volunteers and other financial and charitable support. The group also serves as an educational service and social organization.

Kyle Kazimour, twelve, and his Babi (grandmother), Betty Dostal, both volunteers, fill planters for the Bridge of Lions crossing the Cedar River to connect New Bohemia with the Czech Village and the National Czech & Slovak Museum & Library.

Kyle and friends suggested the name "Kidizens" for their group.

Thousands of dollars and thousands of hours are donated annually. Museums such as NCSML thrive only with such commitment. Volunteers throughout America literally keep the doors open and keep the festivals vibrant in their Czech communities. There are lots of ways to volunteer. Roll up your sleeves and dig into your pockets. Your heritage is that worthwhile.

Volunteers John and Sandra Cermak Hudson suggested revitalization of the Bridge of Lions connecting the Czech Village with New Bohemia in Cedar Rapids. They inspired other volunteers to take action. Projects include banners on the bridge, removing graffiti, repairing and replacing damaged lion sculptures, installing energy efficient lighting, followed by plans to illuminate the bridge's arches, creating a butterfly garden, planting a grove of trees in Osborn Park, and creating a water feature. The Hudsons emphasize, "It is the Bridge of Lions itself that sparks volunteers' imaginations, stretches their expectations, encourages their dreams, and motivates them to act."

The Kidizens, a group of middle school students, have made "Flowers on the Bridge" a reality. Other volunteers restored native habitat along the river, opening the view from the bike trail.

Right:
John and Sandra Hudson are volunteers with a concept.

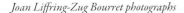

Joan Liffring-Zug Bourret photographs

Authentic Attire, a Source of Delight

Here are two examples of *Kyjovsky Kroje,* both from the town of Kyjov, Moravia, in the Czech Republic. These *kroje* are similar, yet different, when individualized by their owners or the occasion for which each is worn, formal or informal. Versatility is key.

Irene Naxera Hamous

Russ De Hoedt photograph

Amanda (Mandy) Ault

Self-portrait

Irene Naxera Hamous, along with her family, is an avid supporter of her Czech culture, Sokol, and the National Czech & Slovak Museum & Library in Cedar Rapids, Iowa. Irene enjoys wearing her *kroj* at formal and informal occasions, such as festivals. Irene is ever-mindful of the age and delicacy of her *kroj* and wears it carefully, with respect to both of these conditions. This photo of Irene was taken during an informal "Parade of *Kroje*" during Houby Days in the Czech Village of Cedar Rapids. Public wearing of *kroje* is not only a festive and respectful tribute to Czech and Moravian culture, but is also educational for onlookers.

The Hamous family, both adults and children, are recipients of several *kroje* that Irene and Don Hamous acquired during trips to the Czech lands. Because she is also a seamstress, Irene is able to create or supplement *kroje* so that family members may wear different pieces together for the same occasion. Irene wears an authentic *Kyjovsky Kroj,* with blouse and separate collar made of white cotton edged in black and white lace and highlighted with black and white cutwork embroidery. The embroidery is backed by red ribbon, which shows through the cutwork. Irene's vest is of red satin and ecru brocade, highly ornamented with colored beads and sequins in various designs, both on the front and on the back. The gathered skirt is red wool, with yellow and white flowers woven into the fabric. The apron is made of black polished cotton that is heavily embroidered in a colorful, mirrored pattern. The apron hem is trimmed with beautiful, hand-woven bobbin lace. The crowning glory of this *kroj* is the white satin cap, ornamented with woven ribbon and lace, and heavily embellished with hundreds of multicolored beads and sequins. Irene's accessories are a garnet pin, ring, bracelet, and black boots.

Amanda Jane Ault, an attorney living in Oak Lawn, Illinois, is modeling a vintage *kroj* from the area of Kyjov, in southern Moravia. Mandy was crowned the Miss Czech-Slovak Wisconsin State Queen in 2000. At that time she acquired this costume (through Sonka Suvadova-Tostrud and Sonia Riecan of Moja Vlast Folklórny Súbor) and also began to collect other vintage *kroje.* Mandy wears her *Kyjovsky Kroj* at formal events, such as assisting with the Wisconsin pageant and receiving awards or recognition from the Czech- and Slovak-American community. The oldest parts of Mandy's *kroj* are more than 150 years old and are exceedingly fragile. She does NOT wear the costume when she dances with Veselica, a Chicago-based Slovak Folk Ensemble. A full *Kyjov* costume may weigh over twenty-five pounds, and that weight would make dancing more difficult, Amanda explained.

"Each *kroj* is unique and made with much love and patience, generally by a girl's mother, grandmother, and godmother. The women started working on the costume when the girl is born and the owner often adds to the decoration once the wearer herself becomes adept at embroidery and sewing. Through the years, each family adds its own trademark in the embroidery or tatted lace, making the *kroj* even more special," Mandy said.

Mandy's white blouse has large gathered sleeves. Each sleeve has a second sleeve inside the top one, which is laced tightly to the arm to give the sleeve fullness. These sleeves are starched and, on special occasions, are filled with wood chips (Mandy uses netting material to puff the sleeves). The sleeve is tied with accent ribbon (in this case a red ribbon), and the edges are finished off with beautiful, hand-made lace. The lace on Mandy's *kroj* has an intricate pattern of shapes of hearts and flowers. The collar and front-piece of the blouse is also finished with unique Moravian lace. A cotton kerchief wraps around the wearer's neck and is decorated with black embroidery and cut out designs (also in shapes of hearts and flowers). The edges are finished with lace and usually pinned in the front with a decorative brooch. Amanda pins her kerchief closed with a decorative brooch that belonged to one of her Slovak great grandmothers, Alzbeta Polak-Vravis. The vest is made from a red brocade and cotton material, which gives it a rich look. The flowers in the material signify the meadows of the region. White accent panels on the sides of the vest display detailed bead-work and decorative sequins. The vest has an intricate trim with a metallic border. The buttons which close the front of the vest are hand-painted glass. The back of the vest features three circles, made of beads and sequins. White cotton slips, or petticoats, are worn under the skirt to give it a full look. Custom says the more petticoats, the more prosperous the family, and so the women liked to wear as many as they could!

The skirt of this *kroj* is made of red wool. The color red is common in Moravian costumes and is usually associated with the region's significant wine-producing industry. Skirts were made from long strips of three or more yards of material. Because waist ties hold the skirt closed, the waist size is easily adjusted by loosening the ties if the wearer ages or puts on weight. The open seam of skirt is hidden under the apron. Large yellow and white flowers cover the skirt.

Each village in the region has a slightly different pattern and style of flower for its customary decoration. The skirt's waistband is made from off-white linen, with yellow embroidered flowers enhanced by a golden metallic trim. According to Mandy, "Girls usually had several aprons to wear for different occasions. The most elaborate apron was worn for special occasions such as weddings, chris-tenings, and holidays. My apron (a dressy apron) is made from cotton material that has been dyed a rich blue/black. Various lines on the apron were not dyed, so that the white design contrasts with the rest of the piece. The women who created this *kroj* also embroidered the apron richly with a pattern of flowers common to the area." The more embroidery, the more prosperous the family, because its women had time to sit and embroider rather than work in the fields or vineyards. On Amanda's *kroj,* a wide blue embroidered ribbon is worn over the waistband of both the skirt and the apron and is tied in a large bow in back. The floral wreath signifies the wearer is unmarried. Ribbons from various admir-ers may be attached to the back of the wreath, often cascading down her back or over her shoulders as they do in this formal portrait of Mandy. When a girl marries, she no longer wears a wreath of flowers but instead a cap or scarf. Thick black tights and black leather accordion pleated boots, not worn in this photo, are typical for *kroj* of this region, states Amanda.

Czechoslovak-American Marionette Theatre

Helena Krejčí photograph courtesy of the Czechoslovak-American Marionette Theatre

Czech puppetry dates back to the 1800s, when puppeteers traveled town to town, entertaining audiences in rural areas as well as cities. Dedicated to the preservation and presentation of puppetry, both traditional and non, the Czechoslovak-American Marionette Theatre company brings the historic creative marionette traditions of the Czech lands to the stage today. Since its first New York season in 1990, with a cast of sixteen antique Czech puppets, the troupe has created over a dozen original productions and delighted thousands in many nations. In July 2012, during the opening weekend of the new National Czech & Slovak Museum & Library, CAMT presented "The White Doe," or "The Piteous Trybulations of the Sufferyng Countess Jenovéfa." CAMT artistic director Vít Hořejš explained that this production uses "a translation of an authentic text traded orally since the seventeenth century and recorded in the nineteenth." This play features some thirty century-old marionettes and its plot is hilarious. Between the play's six acts, the cast delivers Czech folk songs acappella. Theirs is a Czech puppetry repertoire that combines a scholarly approach to preserving classic puppetry tradition while adapting with delightful, fun, snappy presentations that appeal to audiences of all ages. Contact information for this outstanding team of puppeteers is: Email: info@czechmarionettes.org Website: http://www.czechmarionettes.org

Legend of Svatý Mikuláš (St. Nicholas)

Beginning on December 6, the feast of Svatý Mikuláš, this custom is observed by Czech people. A trio comprised of Sv. Mikuláš, Devil (Čert), and Angel (Anděl), stroll throughout the neighborhood. The devil and angel walk ahead, signaling the approach of Mikuláš, and the devil rattles a chain. Sv. Mikuláš asks each child if he/she has said the prayers and whether the child's behavior has been good or bad. Those who say they have been good are given treats, while the angel records the proceedings in an elaborate book with the use of a quill pen. On Christmas Eve, according to the angel's record, the children receive nuts, candy, fruit, and little gifts if they have been good—and old potatoes or a lump of coal if they have not. Sv. Mikuláš is one of the most venerated of all saints. He was Bishop of Myra, Capital of Lycia, an ancient province in Asia Minor, now Turkey. He is especially noted for his love of children and generosity to the needy and, of course, was the first Santa Claus. *John Johnson photo*

Sv. Mikuláš (St. Nicholas) and his entourage in Cedar Rapids Czech Village during the Old Prague Christmas Market. **From left:** *Hannah Van Deusen, Royal Court Attendant 2010; Brittany Schorg, Devil/Cért; Megan Lehmann, Royal Court Attendant 2010; Sarah Schirm, Miss Czech Slovak Iowa Little Sister 2010–2011; Beth Westlake, Miss Czech-Slovak Iowa 2010–2011; Charles (Chuck) Nejdl, St. Nicholas (Svatý Mikulas); Eric Sindelar, Czech Slovak Prince of Iowa 2009–2010; Emily Nejdl, Angel/Anděl; Abbigail Frerick, Miss Czech Slovak Iowa Little Sister 2010–2011; Marissa Cada, Czech Slovak Princess of Iowa 2009–2010*

United Moravian Societies

The Radost Dancers on Moravian Day, 70th anniversary, 2009

In 2012, United Moravian Societies (UMS) observes its seventy-third year of promoting Moravian folklore by demonstrating the ethnic customs of folk dancing, singing, storytelling, and crafting. This organization was founded in 1939 and consists of forty-one delegates representing twenty Czechoslovakian ethnic clubs and societies. The first Moravian Day was held September, 24, 1939, in Pilsen Park, Chicago. On that day, 26th Street blossomed in the splendor of Moravian costumes, bands, floats, and horses as the great parade progressed from Pulaski Road to Pilsen Park. The event was viewed and applauded by thousands of bystanders.

Thus began the annual tradition of Moravian Day each September, which even after seventy-three years, is a gathering of all Moravian, Czech, and Slovak peoples from the metropolitan Chicago area, as well as many others who travel each year from all parts of the United States, Canada, and the Czech and Slovak Republics. All join together to celebrate their heritage. Today UMS consists of one club. They are still proud to carry on the traditions of the founding members. The weekend festival begins on Saturday evening with a dance, welcoming out-of-town guests. Sunday opens with Holy Mass at 10 a.m., and the two-hour ethnic program begins at 2 p.m. UMS is proud of its five dance groups, which include some 100 dancers, as well as a singing group. The public is always welcome at Moravian Day.

Queen Pageants

From left: *Elizabeth Busboom, Butler County; Laura Shestak, Prague; Alex Cerveny, York and Miss Congeniality Award; Claire Frahm, Omaha Czech-Cultural Club and 2010 Nebraska Czech-Slovak Queen, Oratory, and Best Talent Awards; Kelsey Homolka, Wilber and Runner-up, Best Private Interview, Best* Kroj *and Heritage Awards; Beth Langdon, Clarkson; Erin Spicka, South Central; Marie Bolin, Lincoln; Stefanie Vocasek, Lincoln and 2009 Nebraska Czech-Slovak Queen*   *Sandy Schnackenberg photograph*

Queen Pageants celebrate youth while heralding understanding and appreciation of the heritage, traditions, and culture of Czechs and Slovaks in America. The Nebraska Czech-Slovak Queen Pageant is held annually in June in Clarkson, Nebraska. The year 2011 marked the fiftieth year of this celebration of royalty. Contestants are not beauty queens. Each candidate is judged on strength of character, talent, poise, and "that intangible personality." Contestants in the Nebraska pageant have been chosen as representatives of their particular chapter. Judges are scrupulously selected. There are four aspects of the competition: private interview; oratory award; *kroj* presentation; talent presentation. In the private interview with each candidate, suggested topics include the following: history of Czech-Slovak culture; candidates' personal Czech-Slovak heritage; family genealogy information; candidates' involvement in Czech-Slovak activities; and promotion of Czech-Slovak culture. Rules include: age and single female status, Nebraska residence, and appearance in an authentic *kroj* of her own/local creation (NOT imported). Candidates must be of partial Czech, Moravian, Silesian, or Slovak descent.

The national Queen Pageant is not an exact replica of the Nebraska pageant or any other state pageant. Established in 1987 and held the first weekend in August, the Miss Czech-Slovak US Pageant is in Wilber, Nebraska, because that town is proclaimed to be "The Czech Capital of the U.S.A." Iowa, Kansas, Minnesota, Nebraska, Ohio, Oklahoma, South Dakota, Texas, and Wisconsin have state pageants, wherein state queens are crowned and eventually represent their states at the national level. Candidates from all other states are welcome to participate through the at-large facet of the program.

In Iowa, the Czech Heritage Foundation sponsors Miss Czech Slovak Iowa and the Little Sister Pageant. Candidates for Little Sister are ages six to fourteen years. Little Sisters participate with reigning queens in parades and other events, and the Iowa Little Sister program is inspired by the program as incorporated in the national pageant in Wilber. Little Sisters are also great support systems for Czech-Slovak Queen Pageants. Little Sister programs vary, state to state.

In Cedar Rapids, Iowa, there is also a Prince and Princess Program, sponsored by Czech Heritage Foundation. Begun in 1981, this program encourages both young men and girls, ages fourteen to sixteen, to celebrate their heritage. These young adults compete for the titles and appear in many parades, festivals, and other Czech events throughout the year.

Russ De Hoedt photographs

Above: *Marissa Cada, Miss Czech Slovak Iowa, 2011 – 2012 wears traditional Pilzen* kroj.
Left Little Sisters: *Sarah Schirm, Abbigail (Abby) Frerick, and Cassandra (Cassie) Lehmann*

Texas Czech Heritage and Cultural Center
La Grange, Texas

The Texas Czech Heritage and Cultural Center (TCHCC), Inc., was incorporated in 1997 after statewide efforts to develop a Center facility began in 1995. The City of La Grange, Fayette County, was selected as the site of the Center because of its significance in the history of Texas Czechs. This county has the largest Czech population per capita and the most Czech communities of any county in the state. Fayette County also boasts the distinction of having had more immigrants from the Czech lands of the Austrian-Hungarian Empire settle there in the second half of the nineteenth century than any other county in Texas.

Texans of Czech Ancestry (TOCA) is the umbrella organization that provides representatives from Czech organizations who work to improve and facilitate communication among Czech-founded organizations to support TCHCC and its work.

Groundbreaking for its new building began in June, 2008. On site with this beautiful building is the large Sanford Schmid Amphitheater, overlooking the Colorado River Valley, with stadium seating for about 400. The amphitheater is used for musical productions, weddings, and other festive occasions. Restored buildings in the complex include the Kalich House, which is the home of a the Czech Music Museum of Texas; the Migli House; the Hluchanek-Salas House; the Bucek Store; and the Vasek twin log barns, furnished with artifacts that would have been used in its period. There is also a Wallachian Bell and Belfry from the Roznov region of Moravia. A library, museum, and archives are all located in the new TCHCC building.

TCHCC encourages cultural exchanges, provides space for gatherings of benefit to the Czech people of Texas, encourages study and preservation of the Czech language, fine arts, music, and dance, and educates the public about past and present contributions and the status of persons of Czech descent. A number of organizations support this Center. Volunteers keep the doors open and the festivals vibrant.

Next page: *Lipa, Czech Republic Moravian musicians* **Middle:** *Reception attendees include Czech Ambassador Petr Kolar; James Van Bibber; Rose Steinman; Raymond Snokhous, Honorary Consul General of the Czech Republic, Texas; Pavla Van Bibber; Mrs. Clarice Marik Snokhous; Petr Kolar, Czech Ambassador to the U.S. with his wife Jaroslava; Michelle Barak; Marianne Beran; Retta Slavik Chandler; and others. Pavla Van Bibber baked the cake.* **Below:** *The Cultural Center at La Grange, Texas*

Randy Boyd photography

Czechoslovak Heritage Museum Oak Brook, Illinois

This museum is located inside the home office of CSA Fraternal Life. The library archives historical books and genealogy records, colorful folk *kroje*, hand-cut crystal, and artifacts related to folklore and customs. Founded in 1974 by the Czechoslovak Society of America, the museum proudly displays this magnificent lifesize painting of Tomáš Masaryk astride his favorite mount, Hector, in front of the Presidential retreat at Lány.

Painting is by Frantisek Hornik

The Czech Center New York City

The Bohemian National Hall built in 1896 to serve immigrants at 321 East 73rd Street was sold to the Czech Republic for $1.00. The building, due to its historic past has received city landmark status. Dvořák performed there and Masaryk lectured. Millions of dollars were spent by the Czech Republic goverment refurbishing the historic structure, including a rooftop terrace. Today there are art exhibitions, films, and programs particularly from the Czech Republic. There is a special Havel Library and a full-time director overseeing activities. Over 5,000 people receive their emails about events.

Joan Liffring-Zug Bourret photograph

Czech architects designed a beautiful circular stairway for the Czech Center.

Beautiful Glassware

All Czech Center Museum Houston glass photographs by Kenneth Breaux

From the Ottervik Collection, Czech Center Museum Houston

Bohemian glass-making began in the thirteenth century in the sandy districts of the northwest part of Old Bohemia. The first glass factories were in the forests where there was plenty of wood for fuel. Later, the glass furnaces were moved to areas with coal deposits. Neither World War II nor forty years of Communism managed to destroy the Czech glass industry.

Czechs have had a profound effect on glassware. Glass has been cut, colored, enameled, and engraved. In cut-glass vases there are thousands of cuts. Lead is added to this glass to make it soft enough to cut. Superb creations from these glass artists, including overlay and cut glass, are in royal palaces and modest homes worldwide.

Glassblowers blew the hot liquid with hollow blowing rods or poured it into clay or wooden molds. As the liquid cooled, it hardened. A story tells of a gold watch dropped accidently into a vat, and the molten glass turned red. After that, when a red color was desired, a little gold was added. Other metals added are ferrous oxide for green, cobalt for blue, and manganese for purple.

A glass vase or other object from a mold was cut, engraved, or etched. Perhaps it was painted or gilded. If the glassblower blew a layer of ruby glass over a layer of clear glass in a mold, the ruby glass was engraved to let the clear glass shine through. In another form of artistry, colored enamel (a form of glass) is fused to clear glass and a picture is engraved on the enamel.

Czech glass decorators were first to cut into glass with a little whirling jeweler's wheel. They found ways to engrave beautiful pictures in glass with the point of a diamond, and they were the first to etch faces, flowers, and figures in glass with hydrofluoric acid. Christmas ornaments from the Czech Republic are famous throughout the world. Some are produced using forms more than 1,000 years old, and many have symbolic meanings.

Czech Center Museum Houston

Bill Rosene photograph

St. Wenceslas Chapel

The Czech Center Museum Houston, founded by Bill and Effie Rosene in 1995, is in the heart of the museum district in Houston, Texas, and is one of the city's eighteen fine museums. This Baroque Palace architecture includes Prague International Museum Gift Shop, St. Wenceslas Chapel, Brno Gallery, Presidents Room, Prague Hall, Pilsen Hall, folk art gallery, and Comenius Library. The Chapel is used for religious services, weddings, and renewal of vows. Other venues are used for exhibits, concerts, and community, private, and corporate events. With world-wide membership, this non-profit museum offers innovative programming about the history of the Czech and Slovak people, honoring those who came to Texas, as well as all immigrants who came to America, stayed, and made a difference.

The Ottervik Collection

This collection at the Czech Center Museum Houston has more than 1,289 pieces made in Czechoslovakia between 1918 and 1938. Art glass, pottery, porcelain, and semi-porcelain comprise the collection produced when Czechoslovakia became an independent nation under the leadership of President Tomáš Masaryk. The same glass artisans who made Bohemian, Moser, and Austrian glass produced a portrayal of color in glassware, which brightened the gloom of even the Great Depression of the 1930s. The glass of Czechoslovakia is blown, molded, and cut in many forms including vases, perfume bottles, water sets, boxes, lamps, and baskets. Treasured throughout the world, each piece is marked, attesting to its origin and provenance from the First Republic. The mark is usually found on the bottom and occasionally on the side.

Czech Center Museum Houston collection

Marks include acid etched, ink stamped, molded, stamped in metal, and small metal name plates. The type of mark is of great importance to collectors. (The Czechoslovakian glass of later dates is paper-labeled "Bohemian Glass Made in Czechoslovakia.")

Barbara Špatná, a first generation Czech American from Queens, New York, spoke Czech as her first language and never knew to appreciate her heritage until she met her aunt and uncle from Prague in 1981. She had been raised in an environment that included many Czechs, as well as the Bohemian National Hall and Beer Garden and the famous Zlatá Praha Restaurant (Golden Prague Restaurant), yet the richness of her heritage had evaded her.

Eric Ottervik and Barbara married in 1987, and in 1988 took their first trip together to what was still Communist Czechoslovakia. Thereafter they scoured flea markets, antique shows, and emporiums all over the world, looking for "all things Czech" from 1918 to 1938 when the country was independent. Fifteen years later, when their daughter, Kathleen Ottervik Jameson, returned to Houston, the family came upon the original Czech Cultural Center Houston in a strip mall and met Effie Rosene, Chairman, CEO. Through Bill and Effie Rosene, the Otterviks determined that the new Czech Center Museum Houston was the place to share their collection, which adds to the Museum's presentation of glassware from the collection of James and Danna Ermis in the Brno Gallery. Famous artists' works, furniture from Europe, and other object d'arts are also exhibited.

Vernon Brejcha: Kansas Hot Glass Artist

Hundreds of years ago in the Division of Technical Arts of the University of Prague, courses included painting, woodcarving, and glass ornamentation. Students in all disciplines of study learned about glass to demonstrate aptitude as glassmen or in glassery.

Today, the ancient art of glassmaking is practiced by a modern glassman, Vernon Brejcha, of Lawrence, Kansas. In his Hot Winds Studio there, Vernon creates one-of-a-kind artist hand-blown glass objects and regularly gives tours and demonstrations. Vernon is considered one of the pioneers in the contemporary glass movement. Among the institutions that have collected his work are the Smithsonian Institute, the Museum of Decorative Arts in Prague, the Museum of Contemporary Crafts in New York, the L.A. County Museum, and the Wedgewood Museum in England. Vernon has artwork in more than forty museums in the Czech Republic, Germany, Austria, Japan, and Denmark.

Born in 1942 on a wheat farm near the Czech community of Ellsworth, Kansas, Vernon says the intense heat of glass takes him back to the sun-baked prairies and wheat fields. "It's hard to believe forty years of blowing glass has gone by for a Kansas farm boy whose only introduction to art was comic books," he says. "I was born an artist. It seems there was never a choice for me. My earliest memories are of drawing on the kitchen floor or in the dust of the farmyard. I've tried all media, from paint to metal, but once I dipped a blowpipe into molten glass forty years ago, it seduced me. It's the most demanding material there is. It's magic!"

Photographs by Vernon Brejcha

Glass Fence Posts, named for limestone prairie posts, weighing twenty to twenty-five pounds lean against the bike. Prairie posts weigh hundreds of pounds.

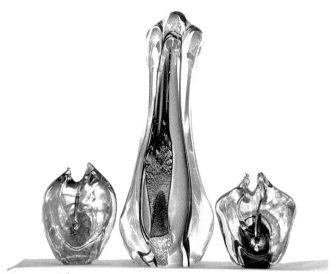

Prairie Objects

Matrix Bowls

Vernon was an art instructor at the University of Kansas for nearly thirty years, and was named professor emeritus there in 2003. He holds BA and MA degrees from Fort Hayes State University and his MFA from University of Wisconsin. In addition to his Kansas teaching, Vernon taught in Wisconsin and Tennessee and has given lectures and presented workshops thoughout the United States, as well as in Japan, England, and Germany. Of glass blowing Vernon says, "I still love the challenge. Guess I'm a visual storyteller. My art objects are about life, passion, and the wonders of nature. The extreme prairie weather, Kansas limestone posts, wheat fields, our Native American past, the origins of life, and vast open spaces inspire me."

Note: *Top center glass is Brejcha's interpretation of a Kansas fence post.*

Distinguished Folk Artist Marj Nejdl

Marj and her granddaughter Emily Nejdl

Marj Nejdl never thought of her talent for decorating eggs as exceptional. This interest resulted from her exposure to a wealth of Czech culture in her childhood, and Marj continued to practice *kraslice,* Czech egg decorating, in adulthood because she wanted to preserve this aspect of her Czech heritage.

Her father was born near Telč, in the Czech Republic, and came to the United States as a young man. Marj's mother, although born in Cedar Rapids, was raised in Czechoslovakia in the lace-making town of Žamberk.

As a child, Marj learned to decorate eggshells, especially for Easter and Christmas decorations, from an uncle who lived next door. She "thought everybody spent hours and hours decorating eggs." She and her uncle perpetrated their own ideas and designs while enjoying one another's company. Marj began egg decorating in earnest during an extended Festival of Czech Arts held at the Cedar Rapids Art Center in 1971. After great success, she began demonstrating her skill publicly and exhibiting her work in area schools, colleges, and festivals. Her techniques include batik, wax resist, pen and ink, scratching, hand painting, and cut-out lace eggs fashioned with a small drill. Her formal arts education included commercial art school in Chicago, so eggs are not her only medium. She works also with wood, ceramics, glass, and "anything with a good surface for painting."

56—

Marj's exceptional artistry with traditional Czech folk art has brought the world to her doorstep in the rural Cedar Rapids area. Since her first public demonstration in 1971, her talent has been celebrated worldwide. She was one of 200 folk artists throughout the United States nominated for a National Fellowship Award through the National Endowment of Arts, and has been listed with the Iowa Arts Council as a Master Czech Folk Artist, receiving the Cultural Heritage Fellowship Award from that organization in 1992.

Marj and husband Ed participated in a two week, 150th birthday celebration for Iowa held during the *Festival of American Folklife* at the Smithsonian Institute in Washington, D.C., in 1996. Selected from some 700 Iowans interviewed for this honor by the Iowa Arts Council, Ed demonstrated strudel and kolache-making, while Marj exhibited her eggs and displayed the techniques of that craft. Other high points of Marj's career include decorating eggs for the Archduke of Austria; former First Lady Barbara Bush; Czech Republic President Václav Havel; Slovak Republic President Michal Kováč; Rita Klfmová, Czech Ambassador to the United States; and Astronaut Eugene Cernan. Two of Marjorie's eggs were displayed at the Smithsonian Institution.

In 2011, Marjorie Kopecek Nejdl was named a Woman of Achievement by Cedar Rapids Waypoint, a most distinguished community honor. "Many woman have the skills and opportunity to help other women, and no real area of support is any more valid than that of helping nurture women's hearts and spirits," read a portion of her tribute.

Joan Liffring-Zug Bourret photo

—57

Daniela and Teresa Mahoney

Daniela Sipkova-Mahoney was born in Prague, Czech Republic, and first experienced traditional egg decorating as a child at Easter. As a young adult, she studied foreign languages and international business in Prague, planning to work for the foreign services of the Czechoslovak government. Due to Communist politics, Daniela was denied opportunities to work in her desired field and in 1980 fled to West Germany with her mother.

In 1982, while working as an interpreter in Frankfurt at a trade show, she met Patrick Mahoney, a businessman from Portland, Oregon. She married him in the United States in 1983. Daniela began a new life in America with an egg.

The egg has symbolized new life and became the perfect canvas to reconnect with her homeland's traditions while opening doors to economic freedom in the United States. She humbly embarked on an entrepreneurial journey selling egg ornaments on sidewalk corners and street fairs in Portland. Today, her business flourishes with distribution across the country.

Daniela estimates that since the spring of 1983, she decorated about 84,000 egg ornaments. Daniela has participated in hundreds of art shows, craft shows, and ethnic festivals nationwide. As a resident artist for Young Audiences of Oregon and Washington and the Regional Arts & Culture Council in Portland, she developed educational programs to teach cultural crafts as part of heritage preservation in the United States. She published several children's coloring and activity books with Czech and Slovak themes and plans to develop multimedia programs to preserve traditional crafts. Most recently she received a grant from the Oregon Folklife Network to teach an apprentice the art of traditional Czech and Slovak egg decorating. Daniela has a bachelor's degree in marketing and a master's degree in social work from Portland State University.

Right: *Eggs decorated by Teresa Mahoney*

Teresa Mahoney was born in Portland, Oregon, in 1987. As a child, she was exposed to cultural crafts thanks to her mother, and decorated her first egg at the age of two. She frequently accompanied her mother to various art and craft events and helped to sell her mother's egg art and eventually her own. In an effort to learn more about her ancestral roots, in the summer of 2009, Teresa decided to participate in the national Miss Czech-Slovak US cultural pageant in Wilber, Nebraska. She won the Best *Kroje* award for the century-old Czech costume she modeled. She also won the Oratory Award after presenting a speech about the

significance of traditional egg decorating in a cultural and personal context. Overall, she placed second in the pageant. Despite the challenges she faced with her older autistic brother, Patrick, and her own diagnosis with Crohn's disease in 2003, Teresa earned a bachelor's degree in business from Loyola Marymount University in 2009 and a master's in digital media journalism from Columbia University in 2012. Teresa has an interest in documentary filmmaking and plans to produce a film about the tradition of egg decorating in the Czech Republic and Slovakia.

Folk Music: Brass, Polka Bands, and Fireflies

Czech music is characterized as fresh, rich, and colorful. Composers Antonín Dvořák and Bedřich Smetana, who wrote their major works in the late 1800s, may be considered founders of the Czech national school of music. Leoš Janáček created operas in the 1900s that demonstrated his interest in Moravian folk music. Most folk music pre-dates the works of these great composers.

Bouncing Czechs at a Tucson performance. **From left:** *Lois Smith, clarinet/alto-sax; Roxanna Baker, accordion; Scotty Welch, trumpet/vocals; John Prokop, tuba/band leader; Dan Duppere, drums; Howard Smith, tenor sax/guitar*

Bouncing Czechs: Tucson's Polka Band

In Arizona, Czechs bounce! Arizona Czechs do not take a back seat to those in any state. This group has been entertaining Tucson crowds for more than fifteen years, playing traditional music enjoyed in the Czech Republic (polkas, waltzes) as well as music of other central European countries and popular American music of the pre-bebop era, according to band leader John Prokop. They play at mobile home parks, senior communities, fraternal organizations, festivals, Arizona casinos, private parties, and Tucson ethnic clubs. Bouncing Czechs have been especially popular for Southern Arizona Oktoberfests. Their website includes video and musical samples: http://bouncingczechs.homestead.com.

Czech Cultural Enthusiasm Pervades Kramer Sisters' Performances

Photograph by Pete Fiumefreddo

From left: *Sue Prochaska Underwood has a* dudy *(Bohemian bagpipe); Dawn Becwar Mundt, a stomp fiddle* (vozemboch); *and Janet Jeffries Beauvais, a guitar.*

Kramer Sisters' performances combine Czech music with other elements of Czech culture. The group owns a costume exhibit that is displayed at Czech festivals. They use Czech language games and snippets of Czech immigrant stories for educational programming between songs. They perform at Czech festivals, Czech conferences, multicultural events, and sing in Czech. Sometimes the group presents American folksongs such as "Red River Valley" in Czech. Instrumentation for this energetic and talented trio includes button accordion, guitar, banjo, harmonica, violin, and even the *dudy,* or Bohemian bagpipe. Audiences enjoy their horse tail jugs and stomp fiddles, popular in South Bohemia.

These entertainers, all of Czech descent, live in Crete and Wilber, Nebraska. They immerse themselves in studying Czech culture, and regularly add to their presentations. One member, Janet Jeffries, leads tours to the Czech Republic via Doane College in Crete. The name "Kramer" is derived from a tiny town east of Crete, where the trio first performed.

The Fireflies

The *Světlušky* ensemble (pronounced SVYET-loosh-kee) is a youth group in Cedar Rapids, Iowa, that strives to preserve and celebrate folk music as they perform folk songs and dances to music they arrange themselves. *Světlušky* is the Czech word for fireflies. Founded in 2007, this ensemble performs Czech, Moravian, and Slovak folk dances, folk songs, and instrumental folk music from the period prior to the advent of brass bands (pre-1850). The group is under the direction of Donna and Guenter Merkle, who began to seriously study Czech folk music while they were members of Houston International Folk Dancers, a recreational folk dance group. Donna, *Světlušky* director, has a background as a musician, and Guenter in study of international folk dance.

The two-fold goal of *Světlušky* is to entertain and educate. Membership in the group is by invitation and requires of members at least two of the following talents: singing, dancing, or playing an instrument, preferably one typically found in folk ensembles in the old country. Such instruments include violin, clarinet, viola, and bass. Other instruments that may be used are flute, recorder, penny whistle, bagpipes, or *cimbál* (hammered dulcimer).

John Johnson photo

Fireflies: *Hannah Van Deusen, Caitlyn Hoffman, Megan Lehmann, Sarah Schirm, Cassandra Lehmann, Carolyn Barker, Jack Fejfar, Elijah Barker, Morgan Simoneau, Michael Simoneau, Donna Merkle (director), Henry Fejfar, and Micah Van Deusen*

The terms ethnic and traditional are used to emphasize cultural roots of the dance. In this sense, nearly all folk dances are ethnic ones. Folk dance uses traditional music, is learned through observation, formal instruction, and mimicry, and is based on tradition. Some dances, like the polka, cross ethnic boundaries and the boundaries between folk and ballroom. *Světlušky* dance numbers incorporate variations of polka, waltz, schottische, and other dance forms. Some variations are ancient, and most pre-date the works of the classical composers. There is a rhythmic movement called furiant that is unique to Bohemia. It incorporates mixed rhythms with a very specific pattern—so many waltzes, so many pivots. The Czech *beseda,* quite pervasive now in the United States but no longer in Bohemia, was created in 1863 for the aristocracy and is not a folk dance. It is a ballroom dance with four sections and is stylized into a square. It is based on folk dances, but the fourth section is largely based on a partner-changing fad of the 1850s.

Today, Czechs in the Czech Republic and in the United States enjoy country, jazz, and rock. But folk music, with its roots in ancient times, continues to stir the heart strings. Folk music comes from the people as they dance, play, listen, and perform. Therefore, let us add spontaneity and caprice to the attributes of fresh, rich, and colorful. Folk music in our Czech communities is practiced, cultivated, and celebrated by musical ensembles throughout the Czech Republic and our United States. "Although the argument can be made that classical music and folk music influence one another, my personal belief is that folk music had more influence on classical music than the reverse," says Donna Merkle, long-time student of Czech music and director of the *Světlušky* ensemble in Cedar Rapids, Iowa.

Donna's opinion is backed by the fact of the life spans of the big three composers: Smetana, 1824–1884; Dvořák, 1841–1904; Janáček, 1854–1928. The first written collections of folk songs did not exist until the mid-1800s, and folk material existed a long time before these composers were born.

Since most folk music was not written down until the mid-1800s, many melodies are fluid and exhibit small variations from village to village. Obviously folk music is composed, but it is not composed in the same sense as classical music. Further, we have no idea who wrote these earliest melodies. In classical music, on the other hand, the notes are fixed according to the wishes of the composer. When the composer is known, it is a serious offense to change what the composer has written, Donna explains.

Nebraska Czech Brass Band

The Nebraska Czech Brass Band, a twelve-piece ensemble led by Ken Janek, clarinetist, is comprised of ten instrumentalists and two vocalists, and is fashioned after the traditional Czech-style brass bands that feature clarinets with standard brass and percussion instruments. The style, known as *dechovka,* captures the spirit and precision of European bands with performance of authentic arrangements, many coming directly from Czech lands. This Czech Brass Band shows versatility by including traditional marches, dixieland, ragtime, and other popular music in its repertoire, as the occasion dictates. Musicians play with symphony orchestras, wind bands, musical theater, jazz bands, country/western, and rock bands. The Nebraska Czech Brass Band is a re-creation of the former Omaha Czech Brass Band, led by Rudy Dvorak, and formed in the 1960s.

Their mission is to preserve the musical heritage of Czech immigrants with authentic/traditional music format using the full instrumentation of the brass band. This format has European roots from the military and village bands, but also is reminiscent of the late 1800s and early 1900s in the U.S., where nearly every town had its own band. Members of this band proudly aim to represent and share their Czech heritage while also encompassing the earlier traditions of American bands.

2006 photo

Front Row: *Ken Janak, Jr., Leslie Janak, Dean Fornoff, Frank Siedlik, Glenn Koca, and Cheryl Janda* **Back Row:** *Annette Wallace, Warren Reznicek, Jeff Janda, John Kool, Matt Sheppard, and Steve Steager*

Polka, Polka, Polka Your Way in North America

Polka Clubs nationally promote this music we love and provide a forum for the fun-loving dancers, toe-tapping listeners, and orchestras of the polka world. States that sport accordion clubs, polka clubs, and polka bands include Alaska, Arizona, California, Florida, Illinois, Iowa, Kansas, Maryland, Michigan, Minnesota, Missouri, Nebraska, North Dakota, Ohio, Oklahoma, Pennsylvania, Texas, Washington, and Wisconsin.

The polka, one of the most widely known dances, is believed to have been introduced in 1830 by a peasant girl, Anna Slezak, who lived near Prague. She danced it on a Sunday afternoon at Elbeteinitz in Bohemia. The dance was first introduced in Prague in 1837, and then in Vienna, St. Petersburg, and London in years following. Wherever it appeared, the polka achieved extraordinary popularity, a kind of polka-mania, with clothes, hats, and streets named for the dance. Within ten years it had spread throughout Europe and to America. Polka is a Czech word meaning "half," and the polka is danced with a half step. Music is written in 2/4 time. The first three eighth notes are generally strongly accented. The polka is a vivacious round dance, performed by couples. Polka music requires a faster, bouncy tempo, because feet cannot remain in mid-air. Not all polkas are the same, nor are polka bands. But polka bands are plentiful in Texas.

The National Polka Festival in Ennis, a Czech heritage town south of Dallas, is held for three days every Memorial Day weekend. May of 2011 heralded the forty-fifth annual event. Performing polka bands are featured, along with a King and Queen Dance Contest, with original Czech *kroje* encouraged as costumes. There is a spectacular parade, traditions, religious customs, and the tastes, sights, and sounds of the Czech culture. Some eighty Texas polka bands preserve and promote this spritely music in that great state! Bands feature the down-home, country music, its place in Texas music history, and the fun and frivolity of this genre. Bands are from Waco, Houston, West, Fayetteville, Dallas, Ennis, Hutto, Flatonia, New Braunsfels, Corpus Christi, San Antonio, Sunnyvale, and many other towns and cities. Polka compositions range from simple to sophisticated. Some are difficult to the point of rivaling classical music. Minimum instrumentation for a good, authentic polka sound today usually is a combination of the following: accordion or button keyboard or concertina, two clarinets, B-flat tenor saxophone, E-flat alto saxophone, two trumpets or cornets, a tuba or sousaphone, and drum.

Legend of the Stork

If a stork builds his nest on a roof next to a chimney or, better yet, on the top of the chimney itself, good luck will abound for that family! At the birth of Jesus in the manger, a long-legged stork with white feathers and a high crest visited the Infant Child, along with the ox and ass and other animals. They all wanted a glimpse of the Christ Child. Although the stork had no crown or valuable gift for Jesus, he saw that Baby Jesus was lying on a bed of straw with no pillow. Thus, despite the pain involved, the stork tugged at the soft plumes on his breast to make a pillow for the baby's head. Since that time, the stork is considered blessed because it gave part of itself for the comfort of Christ.

In more recent times, the European white stork has become a symbol of childbirth. In generations past, parents generally did not speak of the details of reproduction. Instead, parents told the children that storks, symbols of happiness and prosperity, delivered them! Already on the chimney, it was easy for the stork to whisk the newborn down that chimney into the family living quarters.

Before modern times, a household of children helped the family economic fortunes, instead of detracting from them. Therefore, the more storks and babies the better. Storks have become common birth announcements in Western culture. Spotting a stork on a chimney or one flying in the air is also considered an omen of good luck.

In some cultures, a stork is held as a sacred bird from the legend that one flew around the cross used in the Crucifixion of Christ. Today, Czech homes and businesses might place an artificial stork on rooftops or chimney tops, just for fun!

Drawing by Marj Nejdl

Bohemian Garnets: The January Birthstone

The Czech lands abound with legends. There are ancient and medieval legends regarding the Bohemian garnet, which is popular on Czech national costumes and a favorite gem in Czech and Slovak heirlooms, as well as in modern jewelry.

A fourteenth-century reference to the Czech garnet described it as a pyrope "glowing like a flame" on the helmet of the Syrian commander Aretas. The ancients and medieval people believed red stones like garnets, rubies, and blood-stones were remedies for all kinds of hemorrhages. These red gems, which experts call "dove-blood red," also were believed to have a calming effect, and that they could dispel anger and discord. Many garnets were crushed into a powder to be used in ointments or elixirs to strengthen the heart or as an antidote against poisonous snake bites. Because of their red color, they were associated with love, but they were also worn by widows as a consolation after losing a husband.

Worn by people of all social strata—the nobility as well as urban and rural populations—with or without their medicinal value, garnets are still popular. At the time of the National Revival, they were worn as a sign of patriotism. Among the less wealthy, the garnet was often replaced by a glass imitation called a leon stone.

The Bohemian garnet, from what is now the Czech Republic, is characterized by a deep red color, and is thought to be the most beautiful red garnet in the world. Other garnets come in a variety of colors, from yellow and green to pink, violet, brown, and colorless. The black garnets from the volcanic tuffs near Rome were used occasionally in the eighteenth century for mourning jewelry. A popular technique with garnets historically was to inlay.

Today jewelry featuring the garnet is made by many different companies that try to create more modern designs rather than traditional styles, but the tradition of the Czech garnet has been preserved mainly in Turnov, the seat of the Granát (Garnet) Cooperative.

Metal Cross Grave Markers

Crosses with uplifted spires point the way to Heaven—thus they were popular in cemeteries, especially with Czech Catholics. These grave markers are rich in symbolism. Skulls and crossbones symbolize man's morality. Basic designs include angels, cherubs, crucifixes (crosses with the corpus of Jesus included), crowns of thorns, the Lamb of God, Jesus, and the Virgin Mary.

Fitness with Sokol

Founded in the Czech lands in 1862 by Miroslav Tyrš and Jindřich Fuegner, Sokol is dedicated to the philosophy of "a sound mind in a sound body." Based on the belief that only physically fit, mentally alert, and culturally well-developed citizens can form a healthy, strong nation, the program came to North America with immigrants and has been in the United States since 1865.

From coast to coast, branches such as Sokol Canada in Montreal and Toronto, Sokol Cedar Rapids, Sokol Detroit, Sokol Minnesota in St. Paul, Sokol St. Louis, Sokol NYC, Sokol Omaha, Sokol San Francisco, Sokol Cleveland, and Sokol Texas (Ennis and Houston) are active, with some units as old as 130 years. Physical fitness programs and activities for the young and old(er), music and theater, public and private parties, picnics, and festivals all enrich their communities. Sokol groups host dinners with traditional foods and enjoy *Šibřinky* (Czech costume ball). Many maintain historic buildings that enrich the spirit of their downtown areas.

The word Sokol is Czech for falcon, an expressive symbol. In its earliest history in the Czech lands when political conditions demanded extreme vigilance from Czech citizenry, some Sokol training was militaristic. Today, however, the organization extends its wellness reach as a multicultural and diverse organization dedicated to health and education.

Sokol Greater Cleveland

Built in 1896, Bohemian National Hall in Cleveland, Ohio, lower right, was built to serve as a community hall to meet the cultural, social, and educational needs of immigrants from the Czech lands. Lovingly restored to its original glory, with modern amenities, the hall continues to serve new generations. A new 12,000 square foot gymnasium building, shown top right, was added to accommodate expanded gymnastics programs. Both buildings house the many activities of Sokol Greater Cleveland and showcase the cultural history and traditions of the Czech and Slovak people.

New gymnasium

The historic building houses a library, museum, classrooms, ballroom, and more.

Photos and information from Georgia Maresh

Czechoslovak Society of Arts and Sciences

Scholars and scientists, artists and writers, students, lawyers, people of business interests, as well as many others with family and professional interest in the Czech and Slovak Republics are of interest to the Czechoslovak Society of Arts and Sciences. Founded in 1958 in Washington, D.C., the Czechoslovak Society of Arts and Sciences has been active in major cities around the world since that time. However, after the peaceful Velvet Revolution in what was Czechoslovakia in 1989, the Society began to function through local chapters in the Czech and Slovak Republics.

The Czechoslovak Society of Arts and Sciences is nonprofit, nonpolitical, cultural, and dedicated to the pursuit of knowledge. Free dissemination of ideas and fostering contact among people with common interests is the Society's goal. A newsletter is published for members: SVU NEWS/ZPRÁVY SVU.

On even years, the Society convenes a World Congress, with regional conferences every other year. The first fifteen World Congresses were held in the United States or Canada. Since 1993, nearly all World Congresses have been held in the Czech Republic or Slovakia. Congresses stage presentations of panels, scholarly papers, artistic exhibits, concerts, and social events that provide forums for exchanges of viewpoints. Lectures, seminars, and printed materials are usually presented in English.

The Dvořák Society: For Czech and Slovak Music

Dvořák, Smetana, Janáček, Fibich, Suk, Novák, Ostrčil, Biber, Zelenka, Mysliveček, Stamic, Hummel, Rejcha, Suchoň, Schulhoff, Haas, Krása, Klein, Ullmann, Martinů, Kaprálová—and the list goes on! Many Czech and Slovak composers throughout the centuries, from baroque and classical through romantic periods to modern times, are acknowledged through The Dvořák Society.

Although The Dvořák Society is named for the most famous Czech composer, Antonín Dvořák, it is dedicated to the musical artistry of all Czechs and Slovaks. It is a fact that Czech and Slovak composers have been leaders of musical development for centuries, and the Society promotes this fact. Composers and performers, today and in the past, are encouraged through this Society. Czech and Slovak repertoire by non-native musicians is included in published articles and information regarding all aspects of Czech and Slovak classical musical life.

The Society is based in the United Kingdom, but is international in reputation and relates to members in other countries. The group also encourages interest in composers who deserve more attention. Further, the group organizes social activities and musical trips to the Czech Republic and Slovakia, with participants enjoying exploration of these musical nations.

Fraternal Life in America

By Kathryn (Kitty) Chadima

Fraternal benefit societies are membership groups that unite individuals with a common bond, provide them the ability to secure their families' financial security through a variety of life insurance and investment products, and form one of the nation's most effective and efficient volunteer networks, delivering billions of dollars of direct financial aid and community service to those who need it most. These fraternal groups are basically the oldest and strongest financial and volunteer networks in existence in America today.

—The American Fraternal Alliance, Oak Brook, Illinois

Czechs who came to this country helped start one of the original networks of volunteers in America: fraternal benefit societies that met their needs for financial security and which had the ability to help provide community service. Czechs depended on one another for burial insurance as well as support, fellowship, and a team of lodge members to help serve the local communities. With strength in numbers, they developed the democratic system of government available in America.

Today these Czech-American fraternal societies include Western Fraternal Life Association (WFLA), based in Cedar Rapids, Iowa; CSA Fraternal Life based in Oak Brook, Illinois; the Czech Catholic Union (CCU) in Cleveland, Ohio; Texas fraternals include SPJST Slavonic Benevolent Order of the State of Texas, Temple; Catholic Union of Texas, The KJT; and La Grange; KJZT in Austin. Beginning as Czech or Czech/Slovak, some have expanded their missions, allowing wider membership. Some are strictly religious. The tagline for these and other fraternal societies in the American Fraternal Alliance, based in Oak Brook, is "United in service and financial security," which speaks to the unique duality of the organizations' not-for-profit members. Revenues from the sale of life insurance and benefits fund volunteer efforts: food banks, clothing drives, disaster relief, home builds, military veteran and senior assistance, youth and education projects, and scholarships. The societies are listed below.

Western Fraternal Life Association (WFLA), Cedar Rapids, Iowa, was established in 1897 to provide equitable burial insurance for Bohemian and Slovak immigrants, social activities, and a means of preserving Czech and Slovak heritage. Based in Cedar Rapids since its inception, it is the only fraternal benefit society domiciled in the state of Iowa. Originally known as Western Bohemian Fraternal Life or ZCBJ *(Západní Česko-Bratrská Jednota),* lodges were formed mainly throughout the Midwest, where members still attend meetings and special events. In more recent years, the organization has broadened its mission to include community service of a patriotic, educational, cultural, and social nature. Today, it provides life insurance and annuities, serving 120 lodges in 18 states, with nationwide membership. See wflains.org.

CSA Fraternal Life, Oak Brook, Illinois, is America's oldest fraternal benefit society. Formerly the Czechoslovak Society of America, CSA was founded in 1854 on the principles of equality, harmony, and fraternity. The Home Office in Oak Brook, serves 24,000 members throughout fifty-eight lodges in twenty-one states. In 1982, the society changed its name to CSA Fraternal Life. It moved into its current headquarters in Oak Brook, Illinois, in 1995. See csalife.com.

SPJST, Slavonic Benevolent Order of the State of Texas, Temple, was founded by pioneers of Czech descent in 1897. The focus is on "doing good" for each other and for the Texas communities that SPJST members seek to serve. The objective is achieved through the sale of life insurance and financial services through 105 lodges. In recent years, the SPJST's multi-faceted fraternal program has led to the formation of the non-profit Czech Heritage Museum in Temple, Texas and the non-profit conservation-oriented SPJST Education and Nature Center (ENC) in Fayette County, Texas. The SPJST also supports two non-profit homes for the aged in Taylor and Needville, Texas. See spjst.org.

Catholic Family Fraternal of Texas - K.J.Z.T, Austin, was founded in 1894 with the first mutual aid society in Yoakum, by Ann Jakubik and Marie Yurek with Father Francis Just. At their first meeting, the Society of the Assumption of the Blessed Virgin Mary was formed in the spirit of Christian love, and the desire to be of service to each other. It was at the Convention of the Yoakum and Halletsville Societies in November of 1897, where the Katolickou Jednotu Zen Texaskych, was organized. During the 1978 convention, the name was officially changed to Catholic Family Fraternal of Texas - K.J.Z.T. Since that time the Members of the Fraternal have continued to grow and serve one another as well as their parishes and communities throughout the State of Texas. The Fraternal operates on the lodge system and provides insurance and financial security to Catholics and their families. See kjzt.org.

Catholic Union of Texas, The KJT, La Grange, is a non-profit fraternal benefit insurance society operating under the lodge system with a representative form of government. It was established in 1889 in Bluff, (now Hostyn) by a group of male Czech immigrants. KJT was later incorporated under the laws of Texas the same year. It is licensed and operates only in Texas. The Home Office is now in La Grange. KJT stands for *Katolická Jednotá Texaská.* KJT initially accepted only Catholic men into the Union. In 1979, it began accepting women and all Christians in February 2008. See kjtnet.org.

The Czech Catholic Union (CCU), Cleveland, Ohio. It was founded in 1879 and has fifty local groups. CCU is a member of the Ohio Fraternal Congress, but not of the American Fraternal Alliance. It offers a fraternal benefit life insurance society for persons of the Christian faith. See czechccu.org.

Searching for your Czech Roots

"What is your Czech name?" is a frequent query when we know someone of Czech ancestry with the name "Cyndi O'Brien" (her Czech name/family name happens to be Kula). A lot of name discussion occurs when we are among Czechs.

The most common family name in Bohemia and Moravia is the surname NOVAK (newcomer to an old and established village). NOVY and NOVACEK have similar meanings, and PROCHAZKA (one who wanders) resounds that idea. SVOBODA (a free man) or DVORAK (a farmer having free land) are common also. A person with a small home and little land was CHALUPA, CHALUPNIK, CHALOUPKA; and ZAHRADNIK is a gardener. KUCERA is curly, JELINEK means stag or deer, and KRAL is derived from the noun king. Then STASTNY (lucky—as in Lucky New Year) and KOPECEK (little), and so it goes.

If you are interested in your name, continue with exploration into your genealogy. What are your roots? Here is a promise. If you want to investigate your genealogy, do it yourself. You have the interest, so make the time. As you proceed, others will be encouraged by your accomplishments and want to join the search.

If you want to connect with the Czechoslovak Genealogical Society International, the website is www.cgsi.org. This organization supports research and interest among people with ancestry in the Czechoslovak region as it was in 1918, including families of Czech, Bohemian, Moravian, Slovak, German, Hungarian, Jewish, Rusyn, and Silesian origin, dating back through centuries.

Another great source is Jan Dus and Rev. Jan's Genealogical and Travel Services. His website is www.revjan.com and his email address is rev.jan.services@gmail.com. Recommended by Rick Steves, in his book *Prague & the Czech Republic,* p. 48–49, Jan will help you know a bit about your ancestors (or a lot) and help you search for your ancestral home or for living relatives. Jan offers genealogical research in the Czech Republic, as well as personalized travel in Central Europe and translation services. Translating services could help you with historical documents, old letters, current correspondence, or anything written.

Heritage Tours is operated by Mark Vasko-Bigaouette, who led his first group of tourists into the newly-freed Czech and Slovak Federated Republic in 1992. Along with regularly scheduled tours, Mark arrranges tours for travel agencies and smaller family groups. He also offers assistance in locating family ties. For information about trips with Heritage Tours email Mark or visit his web at mbigaouette@yahoo.com, cstours@gmail.com, or http://czechheritage.com.

How to Start

The Internet is your pal in exploring your genealogy, but before you do that:

1. Make an ancestor chart and fill it out as best you can. Document where you get your information, and continue to work on this document as you find new leads.

2. Talk to family members, especially the elderly. Use a tape recorder or video camera. Look at family photographs, especially the older ones. Label names whenever possible.

3. Search through family documents and Bibles for marriage, birth, and death records, as well as photographs. Copy and record all information.

4. Take your information to family gatherings or contact individual family members and compare notes.

5. Research your family group through federal and state census records as far back as possible.

6. Check county, state, and historical society records for the following: marriages, deaths, probate records, land records, county histories, naturalization and citizenship papers, military records, city directories, old newspapers, and fraternal organization records.

7. Look into church records for marriages, baptisms, and deaths. Look for printed church histories. Check cemetery records.

8. Join the Czechoslovak Genealogical Society International. This group has resources you may not have considered.

9. Join your local city, county, or state genealogical society. Attend meetings. Learn from others.

10. When you feel you have sufficient information to follow, begin your research in the Czech Republic. The government has records. You may want to use private researchers who are more flexible. Check references. Eventually you may want to travel to the region of your ancestral roots.

Samplings of Czech-American Restaurants

Kde se dobře vári, Tam se dobře dári!
Where there is good cooking there is happiness.
—Anna Petrick, Caldwell, Kansas

Czech food is not light and makes no effort to cater to health conscious palates. Know this: a diet brat (if there is such a thing) is not delicious! It is a matter of moderation. Indulge yourself once in awhile with a meal that is hearty, served with gravy and dumplings, and have a few beers as you enjoy the meal. Go back to the lettuce and tuna Monday. Some of the best Czech food in America is found apart from traditional restaurants with a full menu of Czech food. Churches and Czech fraternal organizations all over the country have fundraisers featuring traditional Czech food. Some of these are the greatest, and people travel for miles to enjoy the feasts. These dinners feature menus that serve favorites like pork loin with dumplings, potatoes, and kraut, noodles a variety of ways, goulash, and *kolače*. Festivals also feature Czech favorite foods. In Prague, Nebraska, they annually bake "the world's largest kolache," about the size of a limousine.

And it is all tasty and fun! We have used English for names of dishes, but you may find the Czech language in the recipe section, "A Celebration of Traditional Foods."

Cafe Prague, San Francisco, California
Krusovice on Tap and other great beers—good reasons to lunch or stop after work at this hidden-away, quaint neighborhood bar that is a great spot for conversation and relaxing. Also enjoy goulash, pork, and sauerkraut.

Czech Night at Frankie's Bohemian Cafe, San Francisco, California
The first Friday of every month at 7 p.m. "Bohemian" means everything from menu selections that are South-of-Border to German, to Hungarian—but there is a goulash and the Bohemian spirit thrives.

Schroeder's Restaurant, San Francisco, California
In operation since 1893, Shroeder's has survived earthquakes and fires. In the 1930s, newer management opened the doors of this "men-only" establishment to women, and the newest owners, immigrants from the Czech Republic, have expanded the menu. The restaurant serves German and Czech delicacies including goulash, potato pancakes, Jager steak, European sausages, and Schnitzel. A full-service bar boasts Polka music and live entertainment.

Zina's Restaurant and Bar, Torrance, California
"Authentic Czech cuisine" is the focus, so check out the Z Menu. And this means

řizek, svíčková, segedinský, and *hovězi guláš.* Relax, unwind, play darts, and drink great Czech beers.

Vladimir's Czech Restaurant, Inverness, California
Vladimir's Czech Restaurant has been serving authentic Czech food to residents of Point Reyes, California, since 1960. Among the European delicacies offered in Vladimir's menu are wiener-schnitzel, kielbasa, Moravian cabbage rolls, and roast duck. The restaurant has a banquet facility, outdoor patio seating, a full bar, and a boccie ball court for patrons to enjoy a game or two.

Praha Restaurant and Bar, Longmont, Colorado
Serving authentic Central European cooking since 1977, this menu boasts roast duck and sausage platter, and bread dumplings. The dessert tray is said to be terrific. Atmosphere is quaint and romantic, overlooking the Rocky Mountains.

Old Europe Bistro, Naples, Florida
This establishment rocks to Bohemian/Bavarian specialities. Prague duck with kraut and dumplings highlights an extensive print menu including Czech and German offerings. The Old Europe Bistro has sweet, piquant, stuffed, round, and flat dumplings. Generous portions, reasonably priced. And top the meal off with *livance* (Bohemian pancakes). Outdoor seating.

Bohemian Crystal, Westmont, Illinois
Beautiful cabinets of crystal, lace curtains, and servers in traditional garb highlight the atmosphere of this Old-World Czech restaurant. The Czech Sampler Platter is popular, with fork tender-roasted pork loin, smoked pork, and roast duck served with dumplings and red cabbage. Bohemian comfort food rules here, an Old-World restaurant serving large portions at good prices.

Czech Plaza Restaurant, Berwyn, Illinois
Czech Plaza has been serving Bohemian food for more than forty-five years. Breaded pork tenderloin is a specialty. Stunning decor that includes a beer garden. Prague Cutlet, a mixture of ground beef and pork served with brown gravy is a popular item, as is roast pork with dumplings. A choice and varied beer collection. Even carry-out service, and catering available for large parties!

Klas Restaurant, Cicero, Illinois
A large Czech restaurant, opened in 1924, specializing in *svickova,* goulash, and great rye bread. Four private rooms are available for weddings and parties. Al Capone and George Bush, Sr. are included in famous guests. Generous portions, and wine glasses are filled to the brim.

Bohemian Cafe, Omaha, Nebraska
You start with a basket of rye bread and butter—and proceed to liver dumpling soup, *svíčková* with white wine and sour cream gravy, and on it goes, as you

select from a full menu of authentic European dishes. An Omaha tradition, the Bohemia Cafe is a family-run restaurant with the Kapoun family satisfying patrons since 1924. This cafe exemplifies the immigrant experience.

Cy's Cafe, Dwight, Nebraska

Cy's Cafe is a small family restaurant started by Cy and Evelyn Nemec in April 1961. Cy served as a chef in the Army. He catered many parties attended by President Dwight and Mrs. Eisenhower and Vice President and Mrs. Nixon. He came back after his tour of duty to his hometown, Dwight, to start this business with his wife, Evelyn. This restaurant serves Czech part time, and with a limited menu. Wednesday Noon Lunch Special is roast pork, dumplings, and kraut. Poet Laureate Ted Kooser rarely misses driving the ten miles to enjoy this meal. Janet Nemec, one of Cy and Evelyn's daughters, is the proprietress. Another sister, Sharon, helps during noon business.

Kolac Korner, Prague, Nebraska

Duck to dumplings, kolache, rye bread, and music.

Abie's Place, Abie, Nebraska

Authentic Czech food, baked goods, and music.

Sykora Bakery, Czech Village, Cedar Rapids, Iowa

Sykora Bakery features *houska,* kolaches, cream rolls made with real cream, strudels, and holiday breads in season.

Tábor Authentic Czech Eatery Food Cart, Portland, Oregon

In southwest Portland, Oregon, food carts are popular. Open Mondays through Fridays, they are a great option for hungry folks on the move. Monika and Karel Vitek are called "masters of Czech comfort food" served from their Tábor Authentic Czech Eatery Food Cart. The menu cooked in this cute little red hut includes *bramborék* (Czech style potato pancakes), chicken paprika, goulash, and daily soups such as wild mushroom, garlic, and Bohemia goulash. They are most famous for their own invention, "The Original Schnitzelwich" which is a large and delicious sandwich with schnitzel in the center. *Bon Áppétit* magazine loves it! Tábor also caters and offers cooking classes.

Koliba Restaurant, Astoria, Queens, New York

Czech and Eastern European meals.

Kolache Factory

In numerous cities in Texas; also in Kansas, Colorado, St. Louis, Indianapolis, and Cincinnati offering a new twist to an old-world pastry favorite with not-so traditional pepperoni and mushroom, "South of the Border" jalapeño and cheddar cheese, or bacon, egg, and cheese. Barbeque beef or club kolaches as well. All are portable, or for lunch, or anytime. Also fruits and cream cheese are featured along with croissants, sticky buns, and cinnamon twists.

Zlatá Praha Restaurant, Astoria, Queens, New York

From their website: "Our cozy restaurant is the number one destination in New York City for authentic Czech and Slovak cuisine. Whether it is our traditional hearty dishes, good Czech (or German) beer or our stylish and original folk decor, Zlatá Praha is your perfect escape to 'Europe.'"

You may even run into famous and popular Czech athletes and celebrities, like hockey players (Jaromir Jagr, Dominik Hasek, Petr Nedved, Patrik Elias, Martin Straka, Zigmund Palffy); ice skating world medalist Aja Vrzanova; actors Iva Janzurova, Petr Narozny, Radek Brzobohaty, Lasica a Satinsky, Kaiser a Labus, Marian Labuda, Mirek Donutil, Marek Eben; singers Karel Gott, Helena Vondrackova, Eva Pilarova, Waldemar Matuska, Vaclav Neckar, Karel Stedry, Ivan Mladek, Honza Vycital; super model Pavlina Porizkova; film director Milos Forman, etc., to name a few. You may find the courage to ask them for their autographs or to take pictures with them.

Czech American Restaurant, West, Texas

A great mom and pop restaurant in the little town of West, this is a good place to stop between Dallas and Austin. Sausage and stuffed cabbage combo, sweet and savory sausage, and roast pork are popular, as are Czech fries (lightly pan-fried with onions). Famous for baked goods, especially kolaches.

Prague Restaurant, Toronto, Canada

Located in the natural setting of Masaryktown Park at 2450 Scarborough Golf Club Road, this contemporary Euro-Canadian restaurant offers a wide range of Canadian and European dishes, including their famous Czech-Slovak cuisine.

Interior view of the Prague Restaurant

Beer: The Celebratory Meeting Ground of Bohemians and their Brethren

"What is the National Anthem of the Czechs?" I was recently asked by a patron at the National Czech & Slovak Museum & Library in Cedar Rapids, Czech Village. With the correct answer on the tip of my docent tongue I promptly replied, *"Kde Domov Můj?"* (Where is my Home?) He laughed and said, "Nope, it's 'The Prune Song.'" I countered, "Well, if we're joking around I would agree and add that the close second to the humorous selection is, 'The Beer Barrel Polka.'" To polka to "Beer Barrel" always puts a wide smile on my face. And the celebratory raising of a glass of this brew toasts friends, fun, and the fortunes of those joining in. This beverage, obtained by a process of alcoholic fermentation from cereals, hops, and water, has a history that extends back several thousand years. Barley, grapes, corn, rice, mild ales to heavy stouts, dark, light, draught, or bottled. Your choice!

The Czech Republic is not the greatest beer-producing nation, if liquid bulk be taken as a criterion. Neither will the Czechs come in first with consumption per person, however, Czech beer is always quality. Now, my favorite Czech brew is Krušovice Beer, from The Královský Pivovar Krušovice (The Royal Brewery of Krušovice), one of the oldest breweries in the Czech Republic. This brewery was established in 1517 when the aristocracy brewed beer on their own farms. Jiri Birka, from Nasile, offered to sell the brewery to Emperor Rudolf II in 1581, and two years later the purchase was made. Even though the brewery was devastated by mercenaries during the Thirty Years War, beer production has successfully been maintained. This war was not the only crook in the road for breweries. Anhauser Busch and the Czech company Budweiser Budar engaged in controversy over the rights to the name Budweiser.

Carl Conrad and his friend Adolphus Busch created a Bohemian-style lager in 1876, after taking a trip abroad. Bohemian brewers were known for naming their beer after their town of origination with an "er" added after the name of the town. For example, beers produced in Pilzen were named pilsners. Conrad and Busch visited a town called Budweis which was also well known for its breweries. The beers developed there were known as Budweiser, which refers to the original Czech beer, Budweiser Budvar. Some European countries refer to the American Budweiser beer as Bud but the United Kingdom uses the term Budweiser. In 2008, Anheuser-Busch completed a $52 billion sale of majority interest in the stock to InBev, a Belgian/Brazilian company formed by the merger of Interbrew (a Belgian beer company) and AmBev (Brazilian beer company). The company is now called Anhauser-Busch InBev and is the world's largest brewing company!

BrewNost, an international beer tasting celebration hosted by NCSML, is customarily held in September or October in Cedar Rapids, Iowa. Along with a variety of premium beers, this fundraiser features savory hors d'oeuvres, Babi's Bakery, a silent auction, live music, a variety of desserts, and hundreds of happy hops-sipping museum patrons. Live music always includes the group's rendition of "The Beer Barrel Polka." In 2011, more than 750 attendees enjoyed the event.

Czech Center Museum Houston added a Czech Beer Fest to its October calendar in 2011 as a fundraiser for the museum. For this first such event, 250 tickets were sold, and the fare included Czech beer, sausage, pretzels, sauerkraut, and kolaches.

"Czech, Please" for that Wine Tab

It's not just about beer! Sometimes it is "Czech, please" when Czech/Moravian wine is served! Vines are thriving in Moravia in the Czech Republic. The country's wines are becoming more well known in international circles. The Danbue in southeast Moravia provides the necessary warmth and moisture for excellent grape crops in the lands that are currently under vine in the Czech Republic. In Bohemia, north of Prague, there are other protected slopes providing a base for smaller vineyards.

A history of wine making goes back to the thirteenth and fourteenth centuries when Czech Prince Bořivoj planted the first vineyards. High quality reds and white wines are becoming more and more popular, with wine makers and drinkers alike.

In the Middle Ages, the water was unsafe to drink so Moravians drank wine. But today Czechs and Czech Moravians are celebrating with wines. In Houston, "Try Moravian" has been the theme for a wine tasting fundraiser of the Czech Center Museum Houston.

A Celebration of Traditional Foods and Recipes

Illustration by
Bertha M. Horack Shambaugh
(1871–1953), author and artist

Recipes, with minor editing, appear as originally published in *The Czech Book: Recipes and Traditions,* 1981. Time and place for many of our friends and contributors have changed, but these morsels of legacy remain. It is our pleasure to carry them on for new generations of readers and cooks.

Drawings with recipes are by Diane Heusinkveld.

Meats and Main Dishes

Marinated Beef
Svíčková

This recipe, one of the great Czech meat delicacies, is from Libbie Urban, Fort Dodge, Iowa.

1 large onion
3 stalks celery
1 carrot
1 cup cooked tomatoes
1 tablespoon pickling spice
1 tablespoon mustard
1/4 cup lemon juice
1 1/2 cups water
1 tablespoon salt
6 lbs. beef loin or rump roast
6 slices bacon
4 tablespoons flour
1 pint sour cream

For brine, boil together all but the last four ingredients. Let cool. Cut fat from the beef and remove bones. Cut bacon slices into 1/2 inch strips. Cut slits in beef and stuff bacon into the slits. Place the beef in a deep dish and pour cool brine (reserve vegetables) over to cover. Marinate in refrigerator two days or up to one week. The longer, the more tender and better flavored. Remove meat from brine. Place in a roaster and arrange vegetables around the beef. Add brine until beef is half covered. Bake at 350° F, covered, until tender.

Pour remainder of brine into a pan and boil for awhile. Remove the beef from roaster when tender and slightly browned. Add the boiled brine to brine in the roaster. Beat the flour into the sour cream and mix into brine. Place beef in this mixture and return to oven, baking uncovered until the top of the gravy appears crusty. Slice beef into thin slices, pour gravy over meat, and serve. 2 or 3 tablespoons Worcestershire sauce may be added to gravy if desired. This dish can be prepared in advance and reheated.

Czech Rolled Beef
Ptáčky

John Kubasta, Cleveland, Ohio

2 1/2 lbs. round steak, cut 1/2-inch
  thick
salt and pepper
mustard
1/2 lb. bacon
2 1/2 large dill pickles
2 medium onions
2 tablespoons shortening
3 to 4 cups beef broth
2 tablespoons flour
1/2 pint sour cream

Pound beef well to make thin 5" x 5" pieces. Season with salt and pepper. Spread slices with mustard. Place 1 slice bacon, halved, and 1/4 pickle, cut lengthwise, on each slice. Slice and sauté 1 onion till transparent. Place one slice on each beef slice. Roll the beef "sandwich" around the pickle. Secure with toothpick.

Dice remaining onion and brown in shortening. Place in roasting pan with meat rolls and several cups of beef broth made from beef bouillon cubes. Cover and roast for 1 1/2 hours in a 350° F oven. Baste every 15 minutes with additional broth. Remove meat rolls.

Make gravy by adding flour and sour cream to roaster on stove top. Mix and boil. (Mixture will not curdle.) To serve, pour gravy over the beef rolls. Dumplings are a perfect accompaniment.

Easter Loaf
Sekaná velikonoční

Caroline Hruska Sobolik of Spillville, Iowa, wrote, "At Easter, veal was and is our favorite meat. In the late 1890s and early 1900s, most families in Spillville raised a hog, a calf, and a few chickens destined to be used toward making the Easter Loaf."

2 cups cooked cubed veal
1 1/2 cups cooked cubed ham
10 eggs, well beaten
1/4 teaspoon pepper
1 teaspoon salt
1 tablespoon chopped chives or onions
1 clove garlic, chopped (optional)

Combine all ingredients and stir thoroughly. Pour into greased 8" x 8" pan. Bake 45 minutes to 1 hour at 300° F. Cut into squares. Serve warm with celery sticks, or cold with mustard for snacking.

Boiled Beef
with Dill Pickle Gravy
Vařené hovězí maso s koprovou omáčkou

Rose and Lumir Vondracek

2 lbs. beef tip (or other beef cut), sliced
3 1/2 tablespoons butter
5 tablespoons flour
2 1/2 cups beef broth
3 medium dill pickles, sliced thin
1 teaspoon finely chopped dill (optional)
2 1/2 tablespoons white vinegar
salt and pepper to taste

Boil the sliced beef about 2 hours, or until tender. Melt the butter and mix with the flour. Fry to make light golden roux, add to beef broth along with pickles, vinegar, and dill (optional). Cook for about 5 minutes, or until the gravy thickens. Stir constantly to prevent lumping. Season with salt and pepper to taste. Pour the hot gravy over the sliced beef. Serve with bread dumplings. Use the remaining broth to make delicious beef soup.

Veal Ragout
with Caraway Seeds
Dušené telecí maso na kmínu

Helen Secl, Cedar Rapids, Iowa

2 lbs. boneless shoulder of veal, cut into 1" cubes
ground black pepper and salt
3 tablespoons butter
1/2 cup finely chopped onion
2 tablespoons flour
1 1/2 tablespoons caraway seed
1 1/2 cups chicken stock
1 cup thinly sliced mushrooms

Sprinkle veal cubes with salt and a few grindings of pepper. In a 10" or 12" skillet, over medium heat, melt butter, add onion and sauté 6 to 8 minutes or until translucent. Stir in the veal cubes and sprinkle with flour and caraway seed. Stir to coat the veal evenly with the mixture. Cover tightly and cook over a low heat for 10 minutes, shaking the pan every now and then to keep the veal from sticking.

Stir in the stock, bring to a boil and reduce heat to low. Add the mushrooms, cover and simmer for 1 hour, or until veal is tender. Add more stock by the tablespoon if the veal seems too dry or the gravy too thick. Taste for seasoning and serve. Delicious over buttered noodles.

Spareribs and Potatoes
Žebírka a brambory

Janice and David Kralik, Cedar Rapids

3 lbs. spareribs
salt
1 tablespoon pickling spice
1 onion, minced
2 1/2 cups water
4 potatoes, peeled and cut in half

Place meat, salted to taste, in a small roaster. Sprinkle with pickling spice and onion. Add water, cover, and bake at 350° F until tender. About 1/2 hour before meat is done, add potatoes under the meat. If water cooked out, add a little more. Serve with sauerkraut or your favorite vegetable.

European Style Paprikas
Uherský paprikáš

Ann Kenjar, Cedar Rapids

5 large onions, chopped
4 tablespoons shortening
2 lbs. beef or pork, cut in 1" cubes
2 tablespoons paprika
1 teaspoon salt
1 teaspoon pepper
2 cloves garlic, minced
1/4 cup flour
1 cup tomato juice
4 potatoes, cubed
2 cups water
1 cup red wine
1 bay leaf

In a large skillet, sauté the onions in the shortening until brown. Add meat and lightly brown. Add paprika, salt, pepper, garlic, and flour, stirring to coat evenly, and fry for 5 minutes. Add tomato juice, potatoes, water, wine, and bay leaf. Cover and let simmer until potatoes are done.

Sauerkraut and Spareribs
Kyselé zelí a žebírka

Janice and David Kralik

1 lb. spareribs
5 cups water
1 small onion, minced
2 cups sauerkraut (#300 size can)
1 to 2 tablespoons flour

Cook spareribs in water with onion and salt until meat is done. Cut meat into either bite-size pieces or serving size pieces. Measure 2 cups of the broth. Thicken with flour to gravy consistency, then add cut-up meat. This is best when made a day or two ahead and left in the refrigerator so the flavors can blend.

We enjoy this as a side dish with roast turkey, and make a meal with the leftovers.

Pork Roast
Vepřová pečeně

George Radler of John's Cafe was president of the Czech Catholic Union Fraternal Insurance Society, Cleveland.

pork tenderloin roast
salt
1 tablespoon caraway seed
1/2 cup water
3 to 4 tablespoons fat or margarine
1 medium onion, cut in half
1 clove garlic, sliced (optional)

Salt the roast and sprinkle with caraway seed. Place fat up in roasting pan. Add water, fat, onion, and garlic. Cover and roast at 350° F, basting frequently. Add water if needed during baking. When almost done, roast uncovered until meat is tender.

Czech Sausage
Jitrnice

Mrs. Robert E. (Irma) Vanourny, Swisher, Iowa. The spices may be cut in half or omitted.

1 hog head
2 additional snouts
2 or 3 pork hearts
3 pork tongues
4 pig ears
3 tablespoons salt
3 loaves stale bread
6 cloves garlic
1 large onion
1 tablespoon marjoram
1 tablespoon black pepper
1 teaspoon allspice
1 teaspoon ground cloves
1 teaspoon ginger

Boil all the meat with the salt until tender. Debone and grind. Soak bread in water, squeeze dry and grind with garlic and onion. Mix all ingredients together thoroughly. Stuff into sausage casings. Strain the meat broth and simmer the *jaternice* in it 20 minutes. Rinse in cold water and hang on rods to cool. To serve, fry slowly until brown.

D.H.

Pig

Pork Sausage
Jitrnice

Adeline Duda Zuber, South Amana, Iowa wrote, "This family recipe came without any accurate measurements. I decided to write it in pounds and spoonfuls instead of handfuls."

1 pork heart
1 pork tongue
2 pork kidneys, cleaned well
4 pork ears
1 1/2 lbs. pork liver
1 1/2 lbs. pork trimmings or roast
2 lbs. pork skins
1 loaf dry bread, soaked and
    squeezed dry
2 tablespoons salt
1 teaspoon black pepper
2 teaspoons ginger
2 teaspoons cloves
2 teaspoons marjoram
1/3 bulb of garlic, finely sliced into 1
    cup of hot broth

Cover all the meat except the liver with boiling water and cook until tender. Remove from the broth. Cover liver, which has been cut into small pieces, with hot broth and let stand. Remove skin from the tongue. Dice all meat and liver and run through a meat grinder, using a medium blade. Mix well and add the bread and seasonings. Mix well again, adding another cup of broth. Stuff into casings (about 12 feet) and tie off in desired lengths. Prick each one 3 or 4 times with a darning needle. Put in the boiling broth and simmer 10 minutes. Plunge into cold water. Place on a rack to cool. Refrigerate up to 2 weeks or put in the freezer. If preferred, the bulk sausage can be put into containers and kept in the freezer without putting it into casings. Before serving, heat it either in a skillet or the oven until it is piping hot all through.

Pork Goulash
Vepřový guláš

Cherryl Benesh Bartunek, Cedar Rapids

2 to 3 medium onions
1/4 cup lard or shortening
1 1/2 lbs. fresh pork shoulder, cubed
1/2 teaspoon caraway seed
2 teaspoons paprika
salt to taste
dash of cayenne pepper
2 cups water
2 tablespoons flour

Sauté onions in lard. Add pork, caraway seed, paprika, salt, and pepper, brown well. Add 1/2 cup water and simmer in a covered pan until tender (approximately 1 hour). Sift the flour lightly over the meat juices and stir until brown. Add the remaining 1 1/2 cups water and simmer 10 to 20 minutes. Serves 4. Delicious with rice or dumplings.

Pickled Pork Loaf
Huspenina

Mrs. Clarence (Helen Noll) Vlasak's ancestors came to the Dakota territory in 1869. "We keep up the family traditions, one of which is making of Sulc, *whenever hogs are butchered."*

2 lbs. pork hocks
2 lbs. pigs' feet
1 lb. lean pork
1 teaspoon salt
1 tablespoon pickling spice
3/4 cup vinegar
tongue or heart may be added, if
    desired

Wash meat well; cover with water. Add salt and pickling spice tied in cheesecloth. Boil all together until done. If liquid boils down too much, add water. Remove meat from liquid when tender and chop up or put through coarse meat grinder. There should be at least 3 cups of liquid. Place the chopped meat in the liquid and bring to a boil. Add the vinegar.

Let the *Sulc* cool and then pour into a 9" x 9" x 2" pan. Place in refrigerator and let set. Skim off the fat and serve cold, sliced about 1/2 inch thick. Keeps in refrigerator for several weeks but must be covered to keep from drying.

Heart in Sour Cream Gravy
Srdíčka se kysanou smetanovou omáčkou

Leona Netolicky Kaplan, Solon, Iowa

pork or beef heart, cubed (chicken,
    squirrel, or rabbit may also be used)
1 bay leaf
1/2 teaspoon allspice
1/2 teaspoon peppercorns
1 teaspoon salt
1 can evaporated milk or 2 cups heavy
    cream
1 tablespoon flour in 1/4 cup milk
2 to 4 tablespoons cider vinegar

Combine heart and spices in pan with water to cover. Cook until tender. Add milk and then thicken liquid to gravy consistency with flour and milk mixture. Add vinegar according to taste. Add more salt if desired. This is good served over potatoes or bread.

Rabbit Meat Loaf
Sekaná pečeně ze králičí maso

Mrs. George Tichy, Ely, Iowa

1 lb. ground rabbit
1/2 lb. pork sausage
1/2 lb. ground beef
1/2 lb. ground ham
2 teaspoons salt
1/2 teaspoon pepper
1 cup bread crumbs
1/2 cup milk
2 eggs
1 onion, sliced

Mix all ingredients, except onion, and shape into a loaf pan. Top with sliced onion, bake for 1 hour at 350° F.

Rabbit with Prune Gravy
Králičí pečeně
se švestkovou omáčkou

Fern Fackler of Cedar Rapids serves prune gravy hot at Christmas Eve dinner and cold on Christmas Day. Since there were very few sweet things, this gravy was a real treat, and a tradition in the home of Fern's mother and father. If the Czech family lived near a river or a wooded area, Prune Gravy could be served with carp or rabbit.

1 rabbit
1 large onion, quartered
1 bay leaf
2 whole allspice
2 cloves
1 tablespoon salt
12 prunes
1/4 cup raisins
flour
1/4 cup vinegar

Boil the rabbit with the onion, bay leaf, cloves, allspice, and salt. When tender, cut rabbit in small pieces. Cook prunes and raisins in enough water to cover them until tender; drain, saving liquid. Pit prunes and cut up fine. Using reserved liquid, add enough flour to make a nice thick gravy. Add prunes, raisins, vinegar, and rabbit, and reheat if necessary. Serve over dumplings.

Poultry Dressing
Nádivka

Esther Lippert, Cedar Rapids, Iowa

heart, liver, and gizzard from poultry
1 slice of pork or beef liver
1/2 small pork heart
1 large onion, chopped
3 to 4 stalks celery, chopped
3 to 4 whole eggs
1/2 teaspoon sage
1/2 teaspoon salt
1/2 teaspoon pepper
1 pint mushrooms, chopped (optional)
1 loaf stale bread, toasted and
   crumbled

Cook the heart, liver, gizzard, plus extra liver and heart in enough salted water to cover. When tender, remove from liquid and put through the meat grinder. Add celery, onions, eggs, and seasonings. Pour liquid from meat over the bread and add milk to moisten. Mix well.

Combine with meat mixture. Mushrooms may be added at this point. Add more sage or other seasonings if desired. If stuffing a fowl, fill loosely as dressing expands when baking. About an hour and a half before fowl is done, pour rest of dressing around the fowl and finish baking in a 9" x 13" greased pan and bake in 350° F oven for 1 to 1 1/2 hours or until done in the middle.

Roast Goose or Duck
Pečená husa nebo kachna

Virgil and Jitka Schaffer and their son Bob founded the Czech Cottage in Czech Village, Cedar Rapids, in 1975. This charming shop carries a wide variety of imported gifts, antiques, and jewelry.

The Schaffers have been very important to the establishment of the Czech Museum. Jitka and Bob travel abroad at least once a year to buy merchandise and to keep in touch with the relatives there.

1 duck or goose
salt
1 or 2 cloves garlic
dressing (optional) 3/4 cup per lb. of
   bird

Clean, wash, and dry goose or duck. Rub inside cavity and outside of bird with salt and minced garlic or garlic salt. (If using garlic salt, use less of the regular salt.) Stuff lightly with your favorite stuffing, or leave unstuffed. Czech cooks usually leave bird unstuffed and make dressing in another pan.

Place on rack in uncovered roaster, breast side up. Do not cover pan. Roast at 325° F for 40 to 45 minutes per pound for duck or 25 to 30 minutes per pound for goose.

During roasting, pour off accumulated fat in pan. Test for doneness by moving drumstick. If it separates easily from the body in the joint, the bird is done. If browning too fast, cover loosely with foil so steam can escape. However, a crisp, brown skin is desired. A 4 to 5 pound duck serves 4. An 8 pound goose serves 5 to 6.

Chicken Paprika
Kuře na paprice

Sylvia Benesh Courtney, Iowa City

1 stewing chicken, about 4 lbs.
1 medium chopped onion
1/4 cup butter
1/2 teaspoon paprika
salt to taste
dash cayenne pepper
1 1/2 cups water
1/2 cup sour cream
2 tablespoons flour

Cut chicken into small pieces. Sauté onion in butter; add paprika, salt, cayenne pepper, and chicken. Brown chicken on both sides; then add water. Cover and simmer until chicken is tender, 45 minutes to 1 hour. Remove chicken to serving platter. Mix sour cream and flour, then stir carefully into pan. Simmer gravy 5 minutes; do NOT boil because the sour cream curdles. Pour gravy over chicken. Serves 4 to 5 people.

Kasparek, Prague's puppet clown

Savoy Cabbage Deluxe
Výborná kapusta

This recipe was submitted by Max Naxera for his mother, the late Mrs. George J. Naxera.

2 cups potatoes, sliced medium thick
6 to 8 cups savoy cabbage,
  cut medium fine
3 tablespoons minced onion, divided
1 rounded teaspoon salt
1/4 teaspoon caraway seed
2 1/2 cups or more of water, only as
  needed to cook vegetables
1/4 cup shortening
2 to 3 rounded tablespoons flour
2 cups cubed salami

Place potatoes in a kettle, add cabbage and 1 tablespoon of the onion. Add salt, caraway, and water. Cook until cabbage is tender. Melt shortening in iron skillet, add 2 tablespoons onion, sauté until soft. Add flour and mix until slightly browned, add liquid from potatoes and cabbage, cooking until it boils gently. Add salami and heat for 1 or 2 minutes. Add to the potatoes and cabbage, mixing gently. Add more salt and a bit of pepper if desired.

Czech Ham, Cabbage, and Noodle Casserole
Uzené maso se zelím a nudlemi

Sharon Spina Benesh, Milo, Iowa

1 small package noodles
3 tablespoons butter
1/2 medium size head cabbage, diced
2 1/2 cups ground ham
2 1/2 to 3 cups milk
3 eggs, well beaten
1/2 teaspoon salt
pepper to taste

Cook the noodles according to directions until just barely tender. Drain. In a skillet, melt the butter and sauté the cabbage until tender. In a 2 1/2 to 3 quart buttered casserole dish, place a layer of half the noodles, then half the cabbage, and all the ham. Then layer the rest of the cabbage and the noodles on top.

Scald the milk and slowly add to the beaten eggs, beating constantly. Add salt and pepper and beat well. Pour over casserole layers and bake at 350° F about 1 hour or until a silver knife inserted in the middle comes out clean.

Pickled Fish
Ryba v rosolu

Janelle Votroubek McClain, Cedar Rapids

raw fish (trout, pike, carp, etc.) cut
  into 3/4" pieces
2 onions, sliced
2 cups vinegar (Rhine or Sauterne
  wine may be used instead)
1 cup water
1 teaspoon sugar
1 teaspoon salt
1 tablespoon pickling spice
2 bay leaves

Bring fish to boil in salted water, then drain. Add onions, vinegar, water, sugar, salt, pickling spice, and bay leaves. Cook until fish is tender. May be canned or placed in refrigerator for 2 to 3 weeks to marinate. During this time bones will dissolve. May be eaten plain or with a sour cream garnish.

Roast Duck
Pečená kachna

Lad's Tavern, Cleveland, Ohio

1 duck
salt
1 or 2 tablespoons caraway seed
1/2 cup water

Wash dressed duck, salt inside and out, rub with caraway seed inside and all over duck; place in roasting pan, add a little water. Roast at 325° F, turning it occasionally and basting frequently.

When done, drain off most of the grease and allow duck to brown at 375° to 400° F. While it is roasting, pierce the skin on the back and under the wings, which allows the surplus fat to escape. This makes the skin crisp. Cut into serving pieces and serve with dumplings and sauerkraut.

Savoy Cabbage and Beef
Kapusta s hovězím masem

Mrs. Julia Pazour came to this country at 23 years of age.

1 small onion, diced
2 tablespoons oil
2 lbs. beef, cut into serving pieces
1/2 teaspoon caraway seed
1 clove garlic
2 potatoes, cubed
1 head of savoy cabbage, chopped
2 tablespoons butter
3 tablespoons flour

In a skillet, sauté onion in oil until transparent, then add beef and brown. Add enough water to cover, along with the caraway seed, garlic, and potatoes, and simmer, covered. When meat is almost done, add cabbage and cook until tender.

In a heavy saucepan, make a roux from the butter and flour, cook and stir until brown, then add to beef and cabbage. Stir well and simmer a few more minutes. Serve with dumplings.

Black Barley Dish
Černá kuba

Mrs. George Tichy, Ely, Iowa, serves this same recipe, adding 1/4 teaspoon caraway seed and 2 cloves garlic. The completed dish is served with sauerkraut.

This dish was also submitted by Lenore A. Topinka, Cedar Rapids, who adds 1/2 teaspoon caraway seed and 1 teaspoon parsley flakes instead of sage and majoram.

Mrs. Lumir Kopecky, Cedar Rapids, relates, "Czech Kuba (without meat) has always been a traditional Christmas Eve dish in the Kopecky family. This goes back to the days when Catholics were not allowed to eat meat dishes the day before Christmas, so Kuba (without meat) was always the traditional dish for Christmas Eve."

1 cup barley grits
2 cups water
1 lb. pork sausage
1 large onion, chopped
1 cup diced celery
mushrooms, 2 cups or as many as you like, sliced or chopped
salt, pepper, sage, marjoram, and garlic

Boil grits until tender and most of the water is absorbed. Brown meat, onion, and celery until tender. Add grits, mushrooms, and seasonings to taste. Place in a medium size flat baking dish and bake at 350° F for 1 hour.

Soups and Stews

Heart Soup
Srdíčková polévka

Irma Mouchka Kelly was a kolache baker for St. Ludmila Parish's annual summer kolache festival in Cedar Rapids.

1 beef or pork heart, cut into
  quarters
1 teaspoon salt
dash of pepper
1/2 teaspoon caraway seed
1 medium onion, chopped
1/2 cup flour

Cover heart with water, add salt, pepper, caraway seed, and onion, and bring to a boil. Simmer for about 1 1/2 hours or until fork comes out easily and heart is tender to touch. Remove heart and dice. Thicken liquid with flour. Add heart and serve at once.

Milk Soup
Mléčná polévka

Times were bleak for many early Czech settlers, and Mrs. Charles (Martha) Krejci of Cedar Rapids often had this as supper fare. There were always cracked eggs to be beaten, and skimmed milk. Cream was sent to a creamery in exchange for butter or a few dollars.

2 cups milk
1 egg
3 tablespoons flour
pinch of salt

Heat milk to simmer (do not boil) in a saucepan with a tight fitting lid. In bowl mix egg, flour, and salt until smooth, then drizzle into the simmering milk mixture. Cover and let stand 5 minutes. Serves 2 generously.

Liver Dumpling Soup
Polévka s játrovými knedlíky

Janice and David Kralik, Cedar Rapids

2 lbs. boiling beef
8 cups water
2 carrots, sliced
1 onion, minced
2 stalks celery, chopped
1 bay leaf
1 teaspoon garlic powder
salt to taste
1 1/2 lbs. beef liver
4 whole saltine crackers (16 squares)
1 1/2 teaspoons garlic powder
1 teaspoon salt
1 egg

Cook boiling beef, water, carrots, onion, celery, bay leaf, garlic powder (1 teaspoon) and salt to make beef broth. Grind liver and crackers. Add garlic powder, salt, and egg, mixing well. Bring beef broth to a boil.

Dip a large spoon into the broth a few seconds to get it hot. Then dip up a spoonful of the liver mixture, put spoon back into the broth before turning it over. (The liver dumpling should slide off the spoon in one piece. If not, warm the spoon in the hot broth a little longer.) Repeat this procedure until all the liver mixture has been put into the soup. Simmer for 20 minutes. Best when served the next day.

This is a good recipe for people who do not like liver as it takes on the beefy taste of the broth.

Old Fashioned Bean Soup
Zastaralý fazolová polévka

Mrs. Emil Votroubek, Cedar Rapids

1 ham bone
1 1/2 cups dry northern beans
2 medium potatoes, diced
1 medium onion, diced
3 slices bacon
2 tablespoons flour
salt and pepper to taste

Wash beans and place in a large pan with ham bone, potatoes, and onion. Cover with water and bring to boil. Simmer until beans are well done (almost mushy). Add water as needed to keep beans covered. Dice bacon and fry in a medium size skillet to crisp. Add flour, stirring until lightly browned. Add 2 to 3 cups of cooked bean soup to skillet, stirring while it thickens. Pour into soup pot and mix well, adding salt and pepper to taste. Vinegar or catsup may be added to servings at the table, if desired.

Good Nutrition Soup
Dobrá výživná polévka

Mary Hudecek of Protivin, Iowa

3 tablespoons flour
1/4 teaspoon onion salt
3 eggs, beaten
1/4 teaspoon black pepper
2 cups water
1 tablespoon chicken soup base
1/2 teaspoon celery flakes

Brown flour and onion salt in oil in a skillet over medium heat, stirring all the time. Add the eggs and pepper, mixing very well. Stir until the eggs are done. Add water, soup base, and celery flakes. Simmer 6 to 7 minutes.

Serve with rolls of bread for a lunch that's ready in 20 minutes. Serves 2.

Mushroom and Barley Soup
Houbová polévka s kroupami

Ernie Hlas, Cedar Rapids, Iowa

2 tablespoons butter or margarine
1/2 lb. fresh mushrooms
1/2 cup diced onion
1/2 cup diced celery
1/2 cup diced carrot
1 tablespoon flour
3 cups chicken or beef broth
1/2 cup pearled medium barley
1 1/2 cups cooked chicken or beef
salt and pepper to taste

In a 3-quart saucepan, melt butter, add mushrooms, onion, celery, and carrot. Cook over moderately low heat, stirring often, about 10 minutes. Stir in flour, then the broth. Add barley, cover, and simmer until barley is cooked through, about 1 hour. Add cooked diced meat, salt, and pepper. For a creamy soup, stir in about 1 cup of milk. Reheat and serve in soup bowls. Serves 4 nicely.

Sauerkraut Soup
Polévka z kyselé zelí

Rose Bartunek Polehna, Cedar Rapids

2 1/2 pints water
1 cup sauerkraut
1 cup cubed potatoes
1 cup sour cream (1/2 pint)
2 tablespoons butter
3 tablespoons flour
1 egg yolk
salt and pepper to taste

Boil sauerkraut and potatoes in water for 15 minutes. Mix together sour cream, butter, flour, and egg yolk, then slowly add to soup mixture, stirring constantly. Heat thoroughly until well blended, season to taste. Serve with potatoes and rye bread.

Mother Vondracek's Tomato Soup
Rajčatová polévka dle matky Vondráčkové

Vlasta V. Kosek, Cedar Rapids. Her mother's recipe is a favorite of the family. Anna G. Vondracek raised her family first on a farm and then in Cedar Rapids.

16 ounces milk
16 ounces puréed tomatoes
1/2 teaspoon baking soda (prevents curdling)
salt and pepper to taste (only if using fresh tomatoes)

Heat milk and 1/4 teaspoon baking soda in a small saucepan. In a medium saucepan, heat tomatoes and 1/4 teaspoon baking soda. When both liquids reach boiling point, pour together. Do not boil. Soup is ready to serve. Minute rice can be added to the soup if desired, or cooked vegetables such as carrots, celery, etc. Enjoy this family favorite.

Garlic Soup
Česnečka

Bonnie Benesh Samuels, Morning Sun, Iowa

3 cloves garlic (onion can be used for onion soup)
1/2 teaspoon salt
1 1/4 cups boiling water
3 slices rye bread, toasted and buttered

With the back of a spoon, mash garlic with the salt, forming a paste. Pour boiling water over the paste and let stand a few minutes. Pour soup over slices of bread in serving bowls.

Garlic soup is considered a preventative of disease.

Potato Soup with Mushrooms
Bramborová polévka s houbami

Mildred Drahovzal of Cedar Rapids told us, "My father, Frank Libal, was one of the founders of the Cedar Rapids Gladiolus Society. In 1956, he was awarded the achievement medal from the American Home *magazine for his original 'Mildred Ann' gladiolus."*

2 quarts water
4 large potatoes, cubed
1 cup mushrooms (fresh, sliced, or dried)
1/2 stalk celery
1 1/2 teaspoons salt
2 tablespoons butter
2 tablespoons flour

Put all ingredients (except butter and flour) into pot. Cook until potatoes are done. Remove celery and discard. Mash the potatoes in the soup liquid. In separate pan, melt the butter and add the flour, stirring until medium brown. Add to soup for thickening. Serves 6 with rye bread and butter.

Potato Soup
Bramboračka

Mrs. Louis Novak of Spillville, Iowa, remembers her grandparents, Thomas and Marie Fisher Dvorak. "As young people they helped build St. Wenceslaus Church. A bust of Grandpa is at the Bily Museum carved by the Bily Brothers."

4 tablespoons flour
3 tablespoons shortening
2 medium potatoes, cubed
2 cloves garlic, diced
1 medium onion, diced
1/4 cup pearl barley
1 quart water
1/2 cup dried mushrooms
salt and pepper to taste

Brown flour and shortening in heavy iron skillet; cool and set aside. Cook potatoes, garlic, onion, and pearl barley until done. Add the washed mushrooms and browned flour. Cook a few minutes longer. Add seasonings. Serves 4.

Omelette in Milk
Svítek do mléka

Mrs. Frank W. Novotny, Cedar Rapids

2 eggs, yolks and whites separated
3 tablespoons farina or Cream of
   Wheat™
2 cups milk, heated

Beat egg whites until stiff, add pinch of salt. Cream yolks and add to whites. Slowly add farina or Cream of Wheat™ to the egg mixture. The batter should be the consistency of pancake dough. Pour onto hot greased skillet, browning on both sides. Cut into 1/2-inch squares, drop into hot milk and serve.

Cream of Potato and Onion Soup
Zadělávaná polévka
z brambor a cibulí

Kris Barta Jones

1 quart cubed raw potatoes
2 tablespoons butter
3 large onions, thinly sliced
3 tablespoons flour
1 tablespoon salt
pepper to taste
1 stalk celery, finely chopped
1 (13-ounce) can evaporated milk
   with water to make 1 quart
shredded Cheddar cheese

Cook potatoes in a quart of water until well done. Drain, reserving liquid. Mash potatoes well and set aside. Sauté onions in butter until light brown. Sift in flour, stirring until blended. Slowly add the reserved potato water and cook until thick. Mix the potatoes with the evaporated milk and water, then add to the soup. Add seasonings and celery and heat through. Serve with a dash of shredded Cheddar cheese. Serves 4 to 6. The recipe may be cut in half for two generous servings.

Mother's Potato Goulash
Matčin bramborový guláš

Hedvika Konecny Benesh, Cedar Rapids

3 to 4 medium potatoes, peeled and
   cubed
2 large onions, cubed
1 tablespoon caraway seed
1/2 teaspoon salt
1/4 teaspoon pepper
3 pieces fried down pork, cut into
   chunks
2 tablespoons flour
1/4 cup water

Boil potatoes, onion, caraway, salt, and pepper in 1 quart of water. When nearly done add the pork and finish cooking until potatoes are tender. Make thickening using flour and a little cold water (1/8 cup), beat, then add a bit more cold water. Stir quickly into goulash to thicken.

D. H.

Onions

—93

Mother's Browned Potato Soup
Maminčina bramborová polévka zasmažená

Marie Wokoun, Cedar Rapids, Iowa

2 medium potatoes, peeled and diced
1 medium onion, cut fine
1 clove garlic, mashed
1/4 teaspoon caraway seed
1 teaspoon salt
pepper to taste
1/4 cup good meat drippings, beef or pork
2 tablespoons flour
dash allspice

Combine potatoes, onion, garlic, caraway seed, salt, and pepper. Cover with water and boil until potatoes are soft, then sieve. Save liquid. Brown flour in skillet or oven until a medium brown, add to drippings with a little water, stirring until smooth. Add potato mixture, liquid, and a dash of allspice. If drippings are not available, use bacon bits and bouillon as part of liquid.

Czech Dill Soup
Česká koprová polévka

Mrs. Dennis Dvorak, Cedar Rapids, worked at Sykora Bakery as a young girl.

4 medium potatoes, peeled and cut into eighths
2 cups water
1 teaspoon salt
1 1/2 tablespoons flour
1 1/2 cups sour cream
4 to 6 raw or hardcooked eggs
1/2 cup dill greens, chopped

Cook potatoes in water and salt. Do not drain. Mix flour and sour cream in a small bowl. Reduce heat. Slowly stir cream mixture into potato soup. Add boiled eggs, whole or cut. Cook only until set as over cooking causes curdling. Sprinkle dill over each serving.

Morel Mushrooms with Beef Sauce
Houby s hovězí šťávou

Sheryl Bellon, Cedar Rapids, Iowa

1 pint mushrooms, washed and carefully dried
5 tablespoons butter
1 1/2 teaspoons minced onion
1/2 teaspoon minced parsley
1/4 teaspoon salt
1/8 teaspoon nutmeg
2 tablespoons flour
3/4 cup beef broth or bouillon
1 teaspoon lemon juice (**optional**)

Slice mushrooms and sauté in 3 tablespoons butter with onion, parsley, salt, and nutmeg for about 5 minutes. In separate bowl, blend remaining butter and flour, when smooth add broth. Add this to the mushroom mixture and simmer for another 5 minutes. Add lemon juice if desired. If morels are unavailable, *kozibrada* (goatsbeard) or any fall or spring mushroom may be substituted.

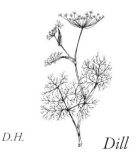

D.H.

Dill

Mushrooms, Cabbage, and Potatoes

Hot Mushroom Sandwiches
Houbový chlebíčky teplé

Vera Krasova Miller, Cedar Rapids

2 cups chopped fresh mushrooms
2 tablespoons butter, softened
1/2 cup mayonnaise
1/4 cup finely diced ham
salt and pepper
4 thick slices French bread
Cheddar cheese, grated

Combine mushrooms, butter, mayonnaise, ham, salt, and pepper. Spread evenly on the four slices of bread. Sprinkle each with Cheddar cheese. Bake in 400° F oven until cheese is bubbly, about 10 minutes. Serves 4.

Mushrooms with Cheese
Houby se sýrem

Mrs. Lumir Kopecky is a second generation Czech.

1 lb. mushrooms, washed and sliced
2 tablespoons butter
1 teaspoon flour
1/2 teaspoon salt
1 cup smetana (sour cream)
2 tablespoons cheese, grated
a few sprigs of dill or parsley, chopped

Sauté mushrooms lightly in butter, stir in the flour and salt. Remove from heat. Blend in the sour cream and sprinkle with grated cheese. Brown under broiler. Serve sprinkled with chopped dill or parsley.

Pickled Mushrooms
Nakládané houby

Sidonia Klimesh, Spillville, Iowa, says, "This recipe is a popular item at potluck meals and also makes a very nice gourmet gift."

1 1/2 cups vinegar
1 cup sugar
1/2 cup sliced onion
mushrooms

Cook vinegar, sugar, and onion until the onion is nearly transparent. Add the mushrooms, stirring carefully. Let come to a boil and simmer for 5 minutes. Pack into small sterilized jars, pour on liquid, and seal.

Mushroom Loaf
Sekaná houbová

Elsie Elias of Cedar Rapids was involved in the Sykora Bakery business for more than 50 years.

1 16- to 20-ounce loaf day-old bread
1/2 to 1 cup milk
1 pint mushrooms, canned, fresh, or cooked
3 eggs, slightly beaten
1/2 cup chopped onion
1/4 cup butter, melted
1/4 teaspoon paprika
salt and pepper to taste

Break bread into 1" cubes; place in a large bowl. Add milk just to moisten. Add remaining ingredients, stirring to mix. If dry add more milk to make a pouring consistency. Bake in a greased 9" x 13" pan at 350° F for about an hour or until set.

Cabbage Rolls
Zelníky

Lester Sykora, Sykora Bakery,
Cedar Rapids, Iowa

4 heads of cabbage
3 tablespoons melted butter or
  margarine
1 teaspoon salt
1 teaspoon ground or whole
  caraway
1/4 teaspoon black pepper
egg wash (1 egg and equal amount of
  water beaten together)
1 recipe of your favorite yeast or
  baking powder dough

Strip outer leaves from cabbage, wash, and drain dry. Shred thinly; cores may be used if chopped fine. Sprinkle cabbage with melted butter, salt, caraway, and pepper. Stir to blend evenly. Put in greased roaster or Dutch oven with lid to keep steam inside. Bake at 350° F for about 1 1/2 hours or until cabbage is tender and tan color. Stir 2 or 3 times so top or bottom will not burn.

Roll dough to about 1/8" thickness and cut into 4" squares. Brush with egg wash or milk. Put tablespoon of filling in center of each square. Bring four corners together and seal seams tightly. Shape into round ball and put seam side down on greased cookie sheet or paper-lined pan. Brush with egg wash. Put in warm draft-free place to rise about 1/2 hour if you use yeast dough. If you use baking powder dough bake at once. Bake at 350° F for 20 to 25 minutes or until golden brown.

Cabbage can be frozen in an inch-deep pan and cut into 1-inch squares as you use.

Cabbage Cakes
Zelníky

Mrs. Arnold J. (Marie K.) Vileta of Tama, Iowa, offers a bit of old Czech philosophy: "To love the good in people around me, and to avoid the wicked, to enjoy my good fortune and to bear my ill, and to remember to forget, that has been my optimism."

2 cups finely shredded cabbage
2 tablespoons butter
1 tablespoon sugar
1/8 teaspoon pepper
1 cake yeast
1 1/3 cups milk
3 eggs
1/2 teaspoon sugar
flour

Stew shredded cabbage with butter, sugar, and pepper. Cool. While cabbage is cooking and cooling, mix batter of yeast, milk, eggs, sugar, and enough flour to consistency of pancake batter. Let rise. When batter has risen and cabbage cooled, combine them. Drop batter by spoon onto a well greased shallow baking pan. Bake in a hot oven on one side, then other, until thoroughly baked. These may also be baked on a hot griddle.

D.H.

Cabbage

Noodles and Cabbage
Nudle s kapustou

Mrs. Josephine Jungman, Cedar Rapids

1 head cabbage
1 teaspoon salt
noodles made from 3 eggs (see
 noodle recipes)
1 small onion, chopped fine
1 tablespoon butter
pepper to taste

Grate cabbage fine, adding salt. Let stand
for ten minutes, then squeeze liquid out.
Cook noodles in salted water, drain, and
rinse in cold water. In large skillet, sauté
onion in butter until golden. Add cabbage
and pepper and sauté until transparent.
Toss with noodles and serve. May be kept
warm in the oven.

Potato Pie
Bramborový kugel

Sylvia Benesh Courtney, Iowa City

3 eggs
3/4 teaspoon salt
1/4 teaspoon pepper
3/4 cup milk
3 large potatoes, peeled and grated
3 tablespoons flour
1/4 teaspoon baking powder
3 tablespoons bacon fat

Beat eggs, salt, and pepper well; add the
milk. Add potatoes, stir in flour and baking powder. Heat bacon fat in large skillet
(iron is best) and pour into potato mixture. Dot with butter. Bake in preheated
400° F oven for 1 hour or until golden
brown. Delicious with roast pork and
sauerkraut.

Konecny's Cabbage Salad
Zelný salát

*From former Konecny's Restaurant,
Cedar Rapids*

6 cups sliced cabbage
1 cup finely sliced carrot
1/4 cup sugar
1/2 teaspoon salt
1/4 teaspoon pepper
1/2 cup milk
1 cup mayonnaise
1/2 cup buttermilk
1/2 teaspoon celery seed
3 tablespoons minced dry onion
2 or 3 drops Tabasco™ sauce

Mix together cabbage, carrot, sugar, salt,
pepper, and milk. Cover mixture and
refrigerate 15 minutes. Combine mayonnaise, buttermilk, celery seed, dry onion,
and Tabasco™ sauce. Pour over cabbage
mixture and refrigerate at least 1 hour
prior to serving. Makes approximately 2
quarts of salad.

Cabbage with
Caraway Seed Butter
Zelí s kmínovým máslem

Marianne Smith, Marion, Iowa

1 medium head cabbage
1/2 inch boiling water in saucepan
1/2 teaspoon salt
3/4 teaspoon whole marjoram leaves
3 tablespoons butter or margarine
1 teaspoon whole caraway seed

Shred cabbage. Place in saucepan with 1/2
inch boiling water, salt, and marjoram.
Cover. Cook quickly until tender, lifting
lid 3 or 4 times to allow steam to escape.
Drain. Add remaining ingredients. Serve
hot. Serves 6.

Caraway Potatoes
Brambory s kmínem

Jessie Stastny, Cedar Rapids, Iowa

4 large potatoes, peeled and sliced
1 small onion, diced
1 tablespoon caraway seed
1 teaspoon salt
2 tablespoons butter

In a heavy aluminum kettle layer potatoes and onion. Sprinkle top with caraway seed and salt, dot with butter. Pour enough hot water over potatoes to barely cover. Bring to a boil, simmer for 15 minutes. Serves 4.

Czech Sauerkraut
Kyselé zelí

Joseph Tesar, Cleveland, Ohio, was president of Karlin Hall, founded in 1936 by Catholic Workmen Lodges. Karlin is a district of Prague and a nickname for Fleet Avenue, a section settled by Pisek and Tabor Czechs.

2 regular cans or 2 packages frozen
   sauerkraut
1 to 2 teaspoons caraway seed
1 large onion, chopped fine
lard
1 tablespoon flour, or more
1 to 2 teaspoons sugar (optional)

Drain liquid from kraut (may be washed and drained again if too sharp), add caraway seed to taste and water to cover. Cook 20 to 30 minutes. Sauté onion in a small amount of lard until onion is light brown.

Add flour, sugar, if desired, and cook 5 minutes or until slightly thickened. Remove from stove and add to sauerkraut and cook for 5 more minutes.

Variation: Mary Barta of Cedar Rapids adds 1/2 cup pork drippings to this recipe for a special flavor.

Homemade Sauerkraut
Domácí kyselé zelí

Leona Netolicky Kaplan of Solon, Iowa, made sauerkraut every year. "It is a fun day. My family comes over and we have a good time preparing for the winter ahead like happy ants. The kraut cutter we use is 50 years old, but the tub is new, being only 20 years old. In 1980 we made sauerkraut out of 280 pounds of cabbage in one day! I grow the caraway seed for the kraut."

40 lbs. of cabbage
scant cup of sugar
scant cup of salt
handful of caraway seed

Remove outer leaves from cabbage, halve heads and remove hearts. Shred the cabbage with a kraut cutter over a large tub. Add sugar, salt, and caraway seed. Mix with hands until juicy. Pack loosely into glass jars, adding juice about level with top.

Add one or two hearts to each jar. Put lids on jars as tightly as possible. Store in basement or similar area. Set jars on newspaper and cover with some in case juice leaks out while sauerkraut is working. Do not disturb the jars if they leak, sauerkraut will be all right. Allow to work 4 to 5 weeks. Makes about 15 quarts. One rule of thumb is that 10 pounds of cabbage makes 1 gallon of sauerkraut.

Noodles and Dumplings

Homemade Noodles
Domácí nudle

Sharon Spina Benesh, Milo, Iowa

1 1/2 cups flour
2 eggs, well beaten
1 teaspoon oil or melted shortening

Put the flour into a small bowl. Make a well in it and into the well pour the well-beaten eggs and oil. Mix this into a stiff dough. Turn out on a floured surface and knead until very stiff. Roll dough out until almost paper thin.

On a clean dry cloth allow to dry partially so dough does not stick together when cutting the noodles. Then cut dough in strips about 2 inches wide. Stack these on top of each other and cut into noodles of desired width. Finished noodles can be boiled in broth or salted water and served as desired. If noodles are not to be used immediately, they should be dried so they do not stick together, and then frozen.

Noodles
Nudle

Helen Horak Nemec, Cedar Rapids

2 cups flour
3 egg yolks
1 whole egg
1 1/2 teaspoons salt
1/4 teaspoon baking powder
1/4 teaspoon vegetable oil
1/4 to 1/2 cup water

Measure flour into a bowl. Make a well in center and add egg yolks, whole egg, salt, baking powder, and oil. Mix well. Add water 1 tablespoon at a time, mixing thoroughly. (Add only enough water to form a ball.) Turn dough into well floured cloth. Knead until smooth and elastic (about 10 minutes).

Cover and let rest ten minutes. Divide dough into 4 equal parts. Roll paper thin. Let dry about 20 minutes on tea towels. Then cut into noodles as desired. Dry about 2 hours. Makes about 6 cups (10 ounces).

Drop Noodles for Soup
Nudličky do polévky

Nancy Barta and her sister Kris Barta Jones are active members of the Czech Village Association. Their father, George Barta, and the family owned the Village's Saddle and Leather Shop in Cedar Rapids, which closed after the flood damage in 2008.

1 egg, beaten
1 cup flour

Mix in bowl with a fork until well blended and dry and crumbly. Drop little by little into boiling soup stock. These noodles take only a few minutes to cook, and are excellent in chicken stock. For a large kettle of soup (8-quart), double flour and egg ingredients.

Liver Dumplings
Játrové knedlíčky

Mrs. Lumir (Rose) Vodracek of Cedar Rapids noted that it is hard to give exact amounts for ingredients because she cooks like her mother did: "handful of this or that."

1 lb. liver, ground (chicken livers are really good in this recipe)
1 cup bread crumbs
1 small onion, grated or diced fine
2 eggs
1 clove garlic, minced
1 tablespoon chopped parsley
pinch of cloves
pinch of marjoram
salt and pepper to taste
soup stock

Mix all ingredients, except soup stock, very well. Drop by tablespoonfuls into boiling soup stock. Cook about 10 minutes.

Sign, Czech Republic

Bread Dumplings
Houskové knedlíky

Mrs. Emil Rezac of Tabor, South Dakota, wrote, "This is the traditional dumpling for the Czechs, as my husband and I noticed on our visits to Czechoslovakia. We were hosted by distant relations with a noon dinner which included soup, meat, sauerkraut, and bread dumplings or potatoes. Dumplings are sliced and look more like oval bread slices. At the end of the feast you take the last pieces of dumpling to sop up the remaining bits of sauce and down the rest of your beer."

1 package of yeast
1 teaspoon sugar
1/2 cup milk, scalded and cooled
1 cup milk, warm
1 egg
1/2 teaspoon salt
3 1/2 cups flour
3 slices white bread, cubed

Mix the first three ingredients, let set for ten minutes. Mix warm milk, egg, salt, yeast mixture, and flour. Add bread and knead. Let rise until double, about 2 hours. Knead again. Divide into 3 long rolls. Let rise about 1/2 hour. Drop one at a time into large kettle of boiling water. Boil about 15 minutes. Remove with slotted spoons onto buttered pan, keep warm. To serve, cut each roll into 8 slices using a thread. Serve with sauerkraut, baked pork, duck, or goose. Makes 24 slices, enough for 8 to 10 people. These freeze well; steam before serving.

Grandmother's Baking Powder Dumplings
Babiččiny kypřicí práškové knedlíky

Dorothy and Ray Snitil were well known for their crafts and woodworking. This recipe was given to Dorothy by Mrs. Albert Fisher, who had learned it from her grandmother.

1 1/2 cups flour
2 teaspoons baking powder
1/2 teaspoon salt (heaping)
1 tablespoon butter
1 egg
milk

Sift flour, baking powder, and salt into mixing bowl. Cut in butter as for pie crust. Beat egg in measuring cup and add enough milk to make 2/3 cup. Pour into flour mixture, stirring lightly until all flour is moistened. It may be necessary to add a few more drops of milk. The dough should not be sticky. Turn dough onto lightly floured board and knead about 20 minutes.

Cut dough into 4 parts. Knead each about 10 times. Let rise 5 minutes in a warm place. Half fill kettle with water and bring it to a rollicking boil. Drop the dumplings in, cover and boil 14 minutes. Do not lift the cover until dumplings are ready to take out. Cut with a thread.

Never Fail Toast Dumplings
Zaručené houskové knedlíky

Mrs. Stanley Rejcha of Beatrice, Nebraska, offered this recipe from her ancestors in Czechoslovakia.

1 slice bread, toasted and buttered
1 cup flour
1 teaspoon baking powder
1/4 cup milk
1 teaspoon salt
1 egg

Cut toast into little squares. Mix all ingredients together. Make an oblong loaf and let rise for 1 hour on breadboard under an inverted bowl. Put in boiling water and boil 10 minutes on each side or until done. Makes one dumpling about 8" long. Cut with string or knife just before serving. Bread cubes are often used in Czech style bread dumplings. Using buttered toast is a nice variation.

Sign, Czech Village, Cedar Rapids

Cream of Wheat™ Dumplings
Krupicové knedlíky

Mrs. Harry J. (Elsie) Chadima, Cedar Rapids, Iowa, is the daughter of Josef Hajek, who was manager of Svornost, the oldest Czechoslovakian daily newspaper in the United States. Elsie's father, born in Czechoslovakia in 1866, studied law at the University of Prague. He began his newspaper work in Cedar Rapids in 1897, with a daily section "Bestnik Iowsky," News of Iowa. Elsie and her brothers or sister would often walk to the post office in the evenings and mail their father's columns and news to the Chicago offices of Svornost.

While still in Czechoslovakia, Josef became friends with Tomáš Masaryk, who became president of the Republic of Czechoslovakia, and with the composer Antonín Dvořák. Both of these Czech celebrities visited the Hajek family in Cedar Rapids where her father would enjoy walking and philosophizing with them.

2 cups mashed potatoes
1 cup Cream of Wheat™
2 eggs
salt

Mash all ingredients together thoroughly. Form into elongated balls. Boil in salted water for 8 to 10 minutes.

Editor's Note: Elsie Chadima's granddaughter, Kitty Chadima, wrote the essay on pages 70–71 about American fraternal organizations.

Potato Dumplings
Bramborové knedlíky

Joe Kocab, Sr. served as secretary of Cleveland's Karlin Hall, an organization of 5,800 paid members. Joe's hobby is cooking. He also was on the radio as "Czech Voice of Cleveland."

3 1/2 to 4 lbs. potatoes, cooked in skins, peeled and mashed
2 eggs
2 cups flour
1 tablespoon salt

Mix ingredients well until flour is absorbed. If potatoes are very moist possibly more flour will be needed. Remove dough to a floured bread board and roll out. Cut into dumpling size. Makes around 15. In a large kettle bring water and 1/2 teaspoon salt to a boil. Drop pieces into water and boil for 8 minutes.

Variations:

Mrs. Esther Lippert, Cedar Rapids
If leftover potatoes are used, put them through a ricer. Grated raw potatoes can be used but water must be squeezed out before mixing them in.

Rose Pecina Cincara received this *sulanky* recipe from her mother, Mrs. Frances Pecina, who came to this country from Czechoslovakia in 1909. Their food was simple with many meatless meals, so the potato was prepared in many ways— potato dumplings, pancakes, soup, *sulanky,* even saving the potato water for rye bread.

Sulanky is a dessert variation. To make a topping for the cooked dumpling, fry cooked Cream of Wheat™ in a little grease until golden. Stir in a bit of sugar. Then add enough water to make the topping a spreadable consistency. Spread this over each dumpling and dot with butter or sprinkle with a cinnamon/ sugar mixture. A second variation is to reduce flour and use farina and half and half when making the dumpling dough. Then stuff each dumpling with pork cracklings or fruit.

Potato Dumplings
Zemiakové halušky

Elsie Malec, Cleveland, Ohio, served as president of Czech Karlin Hall's Ladies Auxiliary. Her husband, Fred Malec, is a musician.

1 head cabbage, about 2 lbs., finely
   chopped
3 tablespoons shortening
2 small onions, chopped
1 teaspoon salt

Dumplings:
2 large potatoes, grated
1 egg
1 teaspoon salt
3 cups flour, approximately

Have cabbage prepared before *halušky* is made. Brown onion in shortening. Add cabbage and salt and fry slowly until browned, about 20 minutes. Set aside until ready for use. Keep hot. Add egg, salt, and flour to potatoes and mix well. Dough should not be thin. More or less flour may be used according to size of potatoes. Put dough on plate. Use knife to cut off small portion at a time into boiling water. Boil about 15 minutes. Keep stirring to prevent scorching. Drain in colander. Rinse once with water. Do not let *halušky* get cold. Place in bowl. Pour cabbage mixture over *halušky*. Serve hot.

Plum Dumplings
Švestkové knedlíky

Marie Wokoun, Cedar Rapids

3 tablespoons butter or margarine
2 cups flour
2 cups cooked, mashed, sieved
   potatoes
1 teaspoon salt
2 eggs, slightly beaten
plums, washed and dried

Cut the butter into the flour until fine as cornmeal. Add the mashed potatoes, eggs, and salt, mixing until smooth. Roll out to 1/4-inch thickness and cut into 3- to 4-inch squares. Place a plum on each piece and carefully and completely surround with dough. Gently put a few at a time into boiling water, not allowing to boil too vigorously. Cook about 15 minutes. Check often while cooking. These may be steamed instead, if desired. Serve with melted butter, sugar, and cinnamon, or even a little cottage cheese. Some people like them withbrowned and buttered bread crusts.

Hope

"Hope is a feeling that life and work have meaning. You either have it or you don't, regardless of the state of the world that surrounds you."

—Václav Havel

My Mother's Fruit Dumplings
Matčiny ovocné knedlíky

Alma Turechek was Professor Emerita of music at Coe College, Cedar Rapids, Iowa.

1 1/2 cups flour
3/4 teaspoon salt
2 rounded teaspoons baking powder
2 eggs
milk
fruit: blue plums, fresh cherries, fresh
  peaches

Sift flour and salt with baking powder. Make a well in the flour, add unbeaten eggs. Stir well, adding just enough milk to make a stiff dough. Dough should be handled, but too stiff a dough makes the dumplings tough. Turn dough onto floured board, kneading lightly 2 or 3 times. Cut into 4 portions, and roll out into 5- to 6-inch rounds, not too thin. Place 1/2 teaspoon flour and 1/2 teaspoon sugar into center of each round, spreading slightly. Place sliced fruit over flour mixture. Moisten edges of each round with milk or water and bring together to close completely. Handle carefully and do not puncture dough.

Drop into a big kettle of boiling water one at a time until they float. Boil 15 minutes or till done, turning carefully once. Gently lift dumplings onto a platter. Brush with melted butter. Blue plums should be halved and pitted. Cherries should be well drained. Peaches should be sliced. The flavor can be enhanced by cooking some of the fruit to make a thin syrup to pour over dumplings.

Mother's Prune Dumplings
Švestkové knedlíky

Mrs. Wencil (Esther) Lippert, Cedar Rapids, says, "My mother made these dumplings when I was a child. I continued making them and when I married, they were a favorite with the whole family."

2 eggs, slightly beaten
1/2 cup milk
2 to 2 1/2 cups flour, unsifted
1 teaspoon salt
24 prunes

Mix all ingredients, except prunes, together. If necessary mix in a little more flour so dough will not be sticky. Take a teaspoon of dough (the size of a walnut) and pat into a circle on a floured board, enough to cover one prune, pinch dough tightly around prune. Cook in boiling salted water about 15 minutes. Cut one in half to see if done, if not, cook 5 minutes longer. Cut and serve with hot melted butter and sprinkle with cinnamon and sugar. Makes about 2 dozen.

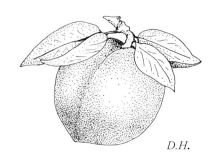

D.H.

Peach

Yeast Breads

Bohemian Rye Bread
Žitný chléb

Mana Zlatohlavek, Cedar Rapids, who came to the United States with her parents when she was 7 years old, says, "We did not have white bread, only rye, so it took us quite a long time to get used to eating white bread."

1 small cake yeast
1 teaspoon sugar
1/2 cup lukewarm water
2 cups warm water or potato water
3 cups rye flour
2 tablespoons melted lard
1 tablespoon caraway seed
3 cups additional rye flour
1 cup white flour
1 tablespoon salt

Combine yeast, sugar, and 1/2 cup warm water and set in warm place for 5 minutes. Add 2 cups warm water or potato water, 3 cups rye flour, melted shortening, and caraway seed. Mix well with a wooden spoon, cover with waxed paper, and let rise in warm place for 2 hours. It will be bubbly on top.

Add remaining flour and salt. Mix well, then knead on bread board thoroughly, kneading in more flour if necessary, so it is not sticky. Form into large ball, return to a greased bowl and sprinkle lightly with flour. Cover and let rise about 1 3/4 hours or until light and double in size.

Turn out onto board and knead out bubbles. Form into 1 round or 2 long loaves and place on floured baking pan. Brush top with melted butter or margarine and pierce with a fork in several places. Let rise about 1/2 hour.

Bake in 350° F oven for about an hour, or until light golden brown. Brush with water when finished baking (harder crust) or with melted butter (softer crust).

Variation:

Mrs. Raymond Vopat submitted a similar bread recipe from the "After Harvest Czech Festival" sponsored annually by the Chamber of Commerce in Wilson, the Czech capital of Kansas. Add 1 tablespoon molasses and 2 cups rye flour with remainder of white flour for a lighter bread.

Bread Sticks
Chlebové tyčinky

Mrs. Floyd D. Herman of Wilber, Nebraska, wrote: "I am a retired farm house wife. The advent of the Wilber Czech Festival triggered my increased interest in our family's heritage."

1 package yeast
2/3 cup warm water
1 tablespoon sugar
1 teaspoon salt
2 tablespoons salad oil
2 tablespoons olive oil
2 1/4 cups flour

Soften yeast in warm water (115° F). Stir in remaining ingredients. Knead about 8 minutes. Let rise until double. Form into bread sticks the diameter of a pencil. They may be any length but if 8" this should make about 50 breadsticks. Put on greased cookie sheets. Brush breadsticks with melted lard, margarine, or beaten egg. Salt generously. Let rise approximately 30 minutes in warm place. Bake 25 to 30 minutes in a preheated 325° F oven. The breadsticks are crisp and tender and keep fresh-tasting indefinitely.

Featherweight Pancakes
Lívance jako peříčko

George Joens, Cedar Rapids, submitted this recipe in memory of his mother, Martha Joens, of Czech descent, who inspired him to help commemorate the Czech people and their heritage.

1 cup dry bread crumbs
3 tablespoons melted butter
2 tablespoons brown sugar
1 teaspoon cinnamon
2 cups milk
3 eggs, separated
1 cup flour
3 teaspoons baking powder
1/2 teaspoon salt

Mix together bread crumbs, butter, sugar, and cinnamon and brown in a skillet, stirring constantly. Pour 1 cup milk over mixture and let stand until milk is absorbed. In a mixing bowl, beat egg yolks and rest of milk, and stir in flour, baking powder, and salt. Mix until smooth, then add crumb mixture. Fold in stiffly beaten egg whites. Bake on hot griddle.

Old-Fashioned White Bread (Made the Modern Way)
Zastaralý bílý chléb

Mrs. Emil Votroubek, Cedar Rapids

2 1/4 cups milk (or 2 1/4 water and
    2/3 cup dry milk)
3 tablespoons butter
5 to 6 cups all-purpose flour
2 packages dry yeast
2 tablespoons sugar
2 teaspoons salt

Heat milk and butter to 120° F. In large bowl, combine 3 cups flour, yeast, sugar, salt, and warm milk. Mix with dough-maker for 3 to 4 minutes. Gradually add enough remaining flour to form a stiff dough. Knead with dough-hooks until smooth and satiny, about 4 to 5 minutes. Dough will not be sticky to the fingers when kneaded enough. Place dough in a greased bowl; turn to grease top. Cover and let rise until double in size, about an hour.

Punch down and divide into 2 parts. Shape into smooth balls, cover and let rest about 10 minutes. Shape into loaves and place in 2 greased 9" x 5" x 3" pans. Let rise until doubled, about 45 minutes. Bake in preheated oven at 375° F for 10 minutes, reduce heat to 350° F and continue to bake for 35 minutes. Remove from pans and cool on rack.

Variations:

Garlic Cheese Bread: Add 1 cup shredded Cheddar cheese and 1 teaspoon garlic powder during first mixing.

Raisin Cinnamon Bread: Add 1 1/2 cups raisins and 2 teaspoons cinnamon during mixing.

Onion Bread: Add 1 package dry onion soup mix during first mixing. Omit salt.

Light Rye Bread: Replace 2 cups white flour with 2 cups rye flour and add 1 tablespoon caraway seeds.

Havel's Motto
"Truth and love must prevail over lies and hate."

—Václav Havel

Grandma Kubicek's *Houska*
Houska dle babičky Kubíčkové

Mary Jen Kubicek Damrow, Cedar Rapids

2 cakes yeast
1/4 cup lukewarm water
1 cup milk, scalded
1/2 cup sugar
1/2 cup butter or shortening
2 eggs
1 egg yolk
1 teaspoon grated lemon rind
1/4 teaspoon mace
1 1/2 teaspoons salt
4 1/2 to 5 cups flour
1/2 cup raisins
1/2 cup almonds
1 cup mixed candied fruits

Dissolve yeast in water. Pour scalded milk over salt, sugar, and butter. Add eggs, lemon rind, mace, salt, 1 cup flour, and yeast mixture. Beat until smooth, adding 2 cups of flour. Let rise until double. Add raisins, almonds, and candied fruit sprinkled with a little flour. Turn onto board and knead rest of the flour into dough. Divide dough in half, then each half into thirds and form into braids. Place on greased baking sheet. Let rise until light. Combine egg white and 1 tablespoon water, brush on braids. Bake at 350° F for 30 to 35 minutes. This recipe makes two large braided loaves of *houska*.

More Havel

"Lying can't ever save us from another lie."

—*Václav Havel*

Easter Yeast Cake
Mazanec

Mrs. Frank J. Stastny of Cedar Rapids, is interested in quilting and crafts, church work activities, Sokol, and C.S.A.

2 cakes fresh yeast
1 cup lukewarm milk
1/2 cup butter, melted
2 egg yolks
1/4 to 1/2 cup light raisins
4 1/2 cups flour
1/2 cup sugar
1 teaspoon salt
1/2 teaspoon grated lemon peel
1 teaspoon vanilla
1/3 cup almonds, finely chopped

Place yeast in a bowl, sprinkle with 1 tablespoon sugar and stir until yeast and sugar are like a liquid. Add 2 tablespoons flour and 2 tablespoons warm milk. Mix well. Cover with cloth and let rise in a warm place 5 to 10 minutes. Add the rest of ingredients and beat with a wooden spoon until thoroughly blended. Turn onto floured pastry board and knead until dough is not sticky. Place back in bowl, lightly oil top, cover with cloth and let rise in a warm place until dough is doubled. Then shape dough on lightly floured board into one large round loaf or two smaller round loaves. Place on well greased baking sheet and brush with one beaten whole egg. Sprinkle with more chopped almonds. Cut a cross in the top of each round with scissors. Let rise a bit longer and bake in a 400° F oven 15 minutes. Reduce heat to 375° F and bake 30 to 45 minutes more, depending on whether you are baking two rounds or one.

Czech Coffee Cake
Česká vánočka

Emma Havlena Barta and her husband, Joseph Barta, were founders of St. Ludmila Parish where Mr. Barta worked as a builder on the church, rectory, and convent in Cedar Rapids.

This recipe was also submitted by Georgiana F. Brejcha of Cedar Rapids. She graduated from Kirkwood at age 64 with a degree as a teacher associate.

2 1/2 cups milk, warmed
2 packages yeast
1 tablespoon sugar
2 teaspoons salt
3 eggs, beaten
1 teaspoon mace
1 cup sugar
1 cup butter, melted
1 cup almonds, blanched and
    slivered
1 cup yellow raisins, softened in warm
    water and drained
approximately 8 cups flour

Combine warm milk, yeast, 1 tablespoon sugar, and enough flour to make a sponge the consistency of pancake batter. Mix well, cover loosely, and let rise 1/2 hour in a warm place. Stir down and add remaining ingredients, working in the flour last. Add just enough flour to make a soft dough; this may be more or less than eight cups. The almonds and raisins tend to pop out of the dough if it is too stiff.

Knead 10 minutes on a heavily floured board or until the dough is shiny and elastic. Let rise until double. Punch down. Now divide to make 2, 3, or 4 loaves, or one giant *houska* can be made. To make a single braid, cut off 1/3 of dough and set aside. Divide remaining 2/3 into 3 equal parts. Roll out the 3 pieces to approximately the same length and width. Set all three side-by-side. Form a braid by beginning in the center and working out to each end. Fold ends together and turn under. Brush with beaten egg and place on baking sheet. Repeat with remaining 1/3 of dough and set the braid firmly on top of the large one. If necessary, use toothpicks or skewers to secure. Let rise until double. Bake in preheated 350° F oven. For small loaves, bake 25 to 35 minutes, for a large one, bake 1 hour.

While warm, brush with melted butter. When cool, braid can be frosted with confectioner's sugar icing flavored with almond extract. Decorate with more slivered almonds, candied cherry halves, etc.

Christmas Sweet Braids
Vánočka

Lester Sykora, Cedar Rapids, Iowa

8 cups flour
1/4 teaspoon mace
1/4 teaspoon nutmeg
1 1/2 teaspoons salt
1 teaspoon dry lemon peel or
    grated lemon rind
1 cup butter
1 cup sugar
2 cups milk, heated
2 eggs and 2 egg yolks
2 envelopes dry yeast dissolved in 1/4
    cup warm water with pinch of sugar
2 teaspoons vanilla
1/2 cup light raisins
1/4 cup or more slivered almonds
1/2 cup candied fruit, chopped fine

Mix flour with spices and lemon rind. Work in butter as you would for pie crust.

Put the cup of sugar into heated milk. Beat the eggs and 2 yolks together. When milk cools, add half the flour. Keep mixing; add beaten eggs, then yeast dissolved in the water.

Add remaining flour until you have a nice, smooth dough. Then add vanilla, raisins, almonds, and candied fruit. Mix well, cover, and let stand in warm place until dough rises to double. Punch down and place on lightly floured board. Divide dough into 9 parts. Roll each piece by hand into 12-inch strips. Braid 4 strips together and put on a greased pan 16 1/2" x 10". Braid 3 more strips together and place on top of the first braid. Then twist together the last 2 strips and place on top of the other 2 layers. Let rise in warm place about 35 minutes.

Egg wash:
1 egg
1 tablespoon milk
1 teaspoon sugar

Beat egg with milk and sugar. Brush braids and bake about 1 hour in preheated 350° F oven. When cool, sprinkle with powdered sugar. This recipe will make two smaller loaves (adjust baking time to 45 minutes).

Bohemian Christmas *Houska*
Česká vánoční houska

Marjorie Hayek, Iowa City, Iowa

1 cup dark raisins
1 cup white raisins
1/4 cup brandy
1 cup milk, scalded
1 cup lard
1 cup sugar
1 1/2 teaspoons salt
1 cup water
1 ounce cake yeast or 2 packages dry yeast, dissolved with 1 teaspoon sugar and 1/4 cup warm water
2 eggs, plus 1 egg yolk
1/2 cup nuts
6 1/2 cups flour

Soak raisins in brandy for 2 to 3 hours. Pour scalded milk over lard, sugar, and salt. Stir until lard is dissolved, add 1 cup water to make mixture lukewarm. Add yeast mixture, eggs, raisins, and nuts. Then add flour. Shape into loaves and bake at 350° F for 1 hour. May be frosted if desired.

Swan at the Charles Bridge, Prague

A Tribute to Havel

"No one of my generation will ever forget those powerful scenes from Wenceslas Square two decades ago. Havel led the Czech people out of tyranny. And he helped bring freedom and democracy to our entire continent."

—*British Prime Minister David Cameron*

Kolaches

Kolaches
Koláče

Helen Horak Nemec worked at Sykora's Bakery.

2 packages dry yeast
1/4 cup lukewarm water
1 tablespoon sugar
1 cup butter or margarine
2 cups milk
2 whole eggs, and 4 yolks
1/2 cup sugar
1/2 teaspoon mace
1 1/2 teaspoons salt
1/2 teaspoon grated lemon rind
6 to 7 cups flour

Dissolve yeast in lukewarm water; add 1 tablespoon sugar and let set until bubbly. Melt butter and add 2 cups milk, heat until warm. Beat the eggs and yolks and add sugar, beating until eggs and sugar become thick. Add warm milk with melted butter. Add yeast, mace, salt, and lemon rind.

Next beat in flour 1 cup at a time. When dough becomes too thick to beat with spoon, turn out on floured board and knead until smooth and silky. Put in greased bowl and let rise in warm place until double.

Turn dough onto lightly floured board and divide into 6 large pieces. Cut each of these into 12 small pieces. Form into walnut size balls (form with your palm). Place on greased baking sheet 2 inches apart and brush each ball with butter. Let rise until almost double in size. Press center and fill with filling. Let rise until light. Bake at 400° F about 7 to 10 minutes. Brush kolaches with butter after you take them from the oven. Makes about 6 dozen.

Crumb Topping for Kolaches
Drobenka

1 cup flour
1/2 cup sugar
1/4 cup butter or margarine
1/4 teaspoon salt (omit if using margarine)
1/4 teaspoon cinnamon

Mix all ingredients together, (using a pastry blender) until crumbly. Use as a topping for kolaches or coffee cakes.

Cherry Filling
Višňová nádivka

1 cup sugar
6 tablespoons cornstarch
1/4 teaspoon salt
2 cans red sour cherries
1 teaspoon red food coloring
1 teaspoon vanilla
1/2 teaspoon almond flavoring

Mix sugar, cornstarch, and salt. Add juice from cherries. Cook and stir until thick. Add remaining ingredients. Makes enough filling for 3 dozen kolaches.

Poppy Seed Filling
Maková nádivka

1/2 lb. ground poppy seed
1/2 cup sugar
3 tablespoons milk
1/4 teaspoon cinnamon, optional
2 tablespoons butter, melted

Combine all ingredients; stir and cook over low heat about 5 minutes. Cool. Use 1/2 teaspoon for each pastry.

Poppy Seed Filling
Maková nádivka

1/2 lb. ground poppy seed
1 cup water
1 cup milk
1 tablespoon butter
1 teaspoon vanilla
1/2 teaspoon cinnamon
1 cup sugar
1/2 cup crushed graham crackers
1/2 cup softened raisins

Add water to ground poppy seed and cook until thickened. Add milk and cook slowly for about 10 minutes, being careful that it does not scorch. Add butter, vanilla, and cinnamon, then sugar and continue cooking for about 5 minutes and remove from burner. Add graham cracker crumbs and raisins for 36 kolaches.

Scones
Vdolečky

This recipe was submitted by Mary Ann and Stanley Studenka on behalf of the membership of the Czech Dancers Polka Club of Metamora, Ohio.

2 cups half and half
1/2 cup sugar
2 packages yeast
8 egg yolks, at room temperature
1/2 lb. butter, softened at room temperature
6 cups flour, more or less, as needed

Heat half and half to lukewarm. Add sugar and yeast and let sit until dissolved (about 10 minutes). Beat egg yolks; add soft butter and blend. Mix in flour, and knead until dough is smooth and satiny and does not stick to a wooden spoon. Cover and let rise until double. Punch down and spoon out dough pieces the size of a walnut. Flatten each piece and add favorite filling. Bring sides over filling and seal well. Place sealed side down, on lightly greased pan, about 1 inch apart. Let rise slightly; then brush with egg yolk mixed with a little milk. Sprinkle with streusel topping. Bake at 350° F until nicely browned, 12 to 15 minutes. Makes 85 scones.

Prune Filling
(or Peach or Apricot)
Švestková, broskvová, nebo meruňková nádivka

2 lbs. dried prunes, peaches, or apricots
1 cup sugar
1 teaspoon vanilla

Cook dried fruit in enough water to cover until tender. Drain, pit, and mash well. Add sugar and vanilla and mix well.

Cottage Cheese Filling
Tvarohová nádivka

1 tablespoon butter
1 lb. dried sweet cottage cheese
1 egg yolk
1/4 cup raisins
1/2 cup sugar
1/4 teaspoon salt
1/4 teaspoon vanilla or lemon flavor

Mix all ingredients together well. Do not prepare until ready to use.

Kolache Dainties
Koláčky

Vilma Nejdl, Ely, Iowa

2 packages yeast
1/2 cup coffee cream, warmed
2 tablespoons sugar
4 cups flour
3/4 lb. butter
6 egg yolks, beaten
1/4 teaspoon mace
1/4 teaspoon salt
1/2 teaspoon grated lemon rind

Dissolve yeast in lukewarm cream; add sugar, and set aside to rise. Put flour into bowl and cut in butter until mixture is crumbly. Add beaten egg yolks to yeast mixture, add spices and lemon rind and add all to crumb mixture and beat until dough is stiff and smooth. Cover and place in refrigerator overnight. The next day, roll out dough 1/4-inch thick and cut into small squares, approximately 2 inches. Fill with choice of filling. Brush each corner with beaten egg, bring corners together and seal securely. Brush tops of the kolaches with beaten egg, place on ungreased pan, bake 10 to 12 minutes at 400° F. Yields 6 1/2 to 7 dozen.

Memories of Christmases Past

By Robert Wachal

When I was a child, relatives and childless friends would gather at our house on Christmas Eve. After I was put to bed, the tree was brought in from the front porch and decorated by the adults while drinking Tom and Jerries. Presents were laid out beneath the tree, and I was wakened and brought down to the living room to open my gifts. It was a grand time for me, of course, and the adults seemed to enjoy it too.

Then came the feast—turkey, a broiled ham, and many trimmings and sides. One favorite was homemade head cheese. That was back in the days when butcher shops carried pig parts—hooves, snouts, ears. It was a grand holiday eve. The next day was Christmas—more feasting. Capon rather than turkey, the latter being not all that tasty back in those days.

But my favorite was baker grandfather's caraway-seeded rye bread. There were mashed potatoes as well as potato dumplings and sauerkraut. The conclusion was my mother's fruitcake, which had spent the prior three weeks being basted alternately with brandy and port wine.

In our house, holidays always meant feasting, either at our house or at my uncle and aunt's. We alternated: whoever hosted Thanksgiving did not host Christmas.

For the adults there were cocktails before (usually bourbon and sweet soda) and beer with the meal—never wine, odd as that seems nowadays. One of the best things about the food was the leftovers, which went on for days, to everyone's pleasure.

One thing you can be sure of about us Czech Americans—we love to eat and drink. There are not many thin folk among us.

Editor's Note:

Robert Wachal is a retired University of Iowa professor. He is the author of the book *Czechs Forever,* published by Penfield Books and a finalist in the Midwest Publishers Association 2011 awards.

Desserts

Poppy Seed Cake
Maková buchta

In the early 1900s, Lester Sykora's father came to America and operated a grocery and bakery in Cedar Rapids and one in Long Prairie, Minnesota. In 1927 he purchased and founded the Sykora Bakery as it is today in the Czech Village. "My father incorporated a lot of the baking recipes his mother used in Bohemia into his formulas which we still use, especially our Bohemian Rye Bread and kolaches."

1/3 cup poppy seeds
1 cup buttermilk
1 cup margarine
1 1/2 cups sugar
4 eggs
1 orange rind, grated
1/2 teaspoon vanilla
1/2 teaspoon salt
2 1/2 cups sifted flour
2 teaspoons baking powder
1 teaspoon soda
2 tablespoons granulated sugar and
  2 teaspoons cinnamon, blended

Soak poppy seeds in buttermilk overnight. Cream margarine and sugar until smooth. Beat in eggs one at a time. Stir in vanilla, salt, and grated orange rind. Sift flour, baking powder, and soda together and add alternately with soaked poppy seeds and milk. Mix to a smooth batter. Pour 1/2 batter into either a 10" angel food or bundt pan, which has been greased and floured. Sprinkle cinnamon sugar mix on batter, then add rest of batter. Bake at 350° F for 35 minutes, or until a toothpick inserted into the middle comes out clean.

Poppy Seed Cake
Maková buchta

Beth Kouba, Yukon, Oklahoma

3 cups flour
2 cups sugar
1 1/2 cups salad oil
4 eggs
1 teaspoon vanilla
1/2 teaspoon salt
1 1/2 teaspoons baking soda
1 (14-ounce) can evaporated milk
1 jar poppy seed filling
1 cup pecans, chopped

Mix all ingredients until smooth. Beat well with electric mixer on medium speed for 2 minutes. Bake for 1 hour and 10 minutes in ungreased 10" tube pan, at 350° F. Cool cake before removing from pan.

Poppy Seed Filling
Maková nádivka

Commercial poppy seed filling may be used for the following recipe.

1 lb. ground poppy seeds
4 cups water
1 cup milk
1 1/2 cups sugar
2 tablespoons vanilla
2 tablespoons butter

Cook poppy seeds and water 10 to 15 minutes. Add milk and cook another 10 to 15 minutes. When done add sugar, vanilla, and butter. This may be frozen when not needed right away. Use 1 1/2 cups in the above recipe.

Christmas Poppy Seed Cake
Vánoční maková buchta

Fern Kaplan Fackler, Cedar Rapids, wrote, "I always looked forward to Christmas time as the food was so delicious, and we were treated to several kinds of baked goods with poppy seeds. My daughter decided that we should have our own Christmas tradition and have this cake for Christmas morning. We have continued this tradition for many years."

12 ounces poppy seed filling
1 cup margarine
1 1/2 cups sugar
4 eggs, separated
1 teaspoon vanilla
1 cup sour cream
1 tablespoon mayonnaise
2 1/2 cups sifted flour
1 teaspoon soda

Cream margarine and 1 cup of sugar together. Add poppy seed filling, and egg yolks one at a time. Blend in vanilla, sour cream, and mayonnaise. Sift flour and soda together and add slowly to poppy seed mixture. Beat egg whites until stiff, slowly adding 1/2 cup of sugar. Beat well, then fold into poppy seed mixture.

Pour into greased tube cake pan which has bottom lined with waxed paper. Bake at 350° F for 1 hour and 15 to 20 minutes. Cool 5 minutes before removing from pan, peel off waxed paper. Sift powdered sugar onto top of cake through a doily or paper cutout.

Nut Coffee Cake
Ořechová bábovka

Marjorie Kopecek Nejdl

5 cups flour
2 packages dry yeast
1/2 cup sugar
1 1/3 cups warm milk
1/2 cup butter, melted
1 teaspoon vanilla extract
1 teaspoon grated lemon rind
2 eggs, slightly beaten
1/2 teaspoon salt

Sift the flour into a large bowl and make a well in the middle. Put in yeast, 1 tablespoon sugar, and 1/2 cup warm milk. Let stand for 10 minutes. Add remaining milk and ingredients. Mix then beat well with a wooden spoon until smooth. Cover and let rise in a warm place until double in size (about 1 1/2 hours).

On a floured board, roll out dough to 1/4- to 1/2-inch thickness. Spread nut filling on the dough and roll as for a jelly roll. Place in a well greased *bábovka* (or Bundt pan) and let rise for another 1 1/2 hours. Bake in preheated 350° F oven for about 45 minutes. Let cool about 5 minutes, then invert onto a plate and powder with powdered sugar before serving.

Havel's Wisdom

"I really do inhabit a system in which words are capable of shaking the entire structure of government, where words can prove mightier than ten military divisions."

—*Václav Havel*

Nut Filling
Ořechová nádivka

1/2 cup sugar
1/4 cup butter, melted
1 teaspoon vanilla
2 eggs, separated
1 1/2 cups finely ground nuts

Cream sugar, butter, vanilla, and egg yolks. Beat well. Beat egg whites separately until stiff, fold into butter mixture. Fold in nuts.

Bessie's Apple Strudel
Jablkový závin

This recipe is from Konecny's Restaurant, which was a traditional family style establishment with its "down home" cooking.

1/4 cup butter, melted
1/4 cup milk, warm
1/4 teaspoon salt
1 egg, well beaten
1 1/4 cups plus 2 level tablespoons flour
4 cups peeled and sliced apples
1 tablespoon butter
1/3 cup raisins
3/4 cup sugar
1/4 cup nuts

Mix melted butter, milk, salt, egg, and flour together and place in a well-floured bowl. Cover and keep warm while preparing apples. Place dough mixture on well-floured pastry cloth and stretch with your hands until pulled paper thin. Spread apples on dough. Mix butter, raisins, sugar, and nuts and sprinkle over the apples. Roll up like a jelly roll and place on a greased cookie sheet, seam side down. Brush top of roll with 1 teaspoon butter or cream. Bake at 375° F for 30 minutes, then reduce heat to 350° F and continue baking until apples are tender. Baste the top with its own syrup, to which may be added a small amount of cream, to keep the strudel from getting a hard crust. Yields 24 servings.

Angel Pie
Andělský koláč

Janelle Votroubek McClain and her husband George were the proprietors of an art gallery and frame studio in Cedar Rapids. They gave a painting by Zora DuVall, artist of Czechoslovakian descent, to the Czech Heritage Museum in Cedar Rapids. Janelle writes of this recipe: "At Christmas time I like to decorate this with red and green maraschino cherries cut to look like poinsettias."

1 cup milk
1/2 cup sugar
2 tablespoons flour
2 egg whites
dash of salt
1 teaspoon vanilla or almond flavoring
1 pie shell, baked
1 cup heavy cream, whipped

Cook milk, sugar, and flour together until thick; cool. Beat egg whites until stiff and fold into the pudding. Add flavoring. Pour into baked pie shell or crumb shell. Cover with whipped cream. Refrigerate 3 to 4 hours. May be frozen.

Great-Grandma Kubicek's Rhubarb Custard Pie
Reveňový nákyp prababičky Kubíčkové

Margaret Z. Kubicek, Cedar Rapids

1 recipe plain pastry (below)
1 1/2 to 2 cups sugar
3 tablespoons flour
1/8 teaspoon salt
2 eggs, beaten
3 cups rhubarb, cut in pieces

Combine sugar, flour, and salt. Add eggs, beating until smooth. Stir in rhubarb. Fill 9-inch pastry lined pan. Adjust top crust. Bake at 450° F for 10 minutes, then at 350° F for 30 minutes.

Plain Pastry:

2 cups flour
1 teaspoon salt
2/3 cup shortening
5 to 6 tablespoons cold water

Sift flour and salt. Cut in shortening until mixture is size of small peas. Slowly add water, mix and press ingredients together until dough holds together. Divide and roll on lightly floured surface to make 2 crusts.

Czech Tradition

City or town squares were used in the evening hours as promenades for local people and especially for young lovers.

Nice and Easy Nut Roll
Ořechová rohlíčky

Submitted by Mary Ann and Stanley Studenka on behalf of the Czech Dancers Polka Club, Metamora, Ohio.

2 packages dry yeast
1/2 cup milk, warmed
6 cups flour
3 tablespoons sugar
1 tablespoon salt
2 cups butter
1 cup sour cream
3 eggs, beaten

In small bowl, dissolve yeast in warm milk, set aside. In large bowl combine flour, sugar, salt, butter, sour cream, and eggs. Beat well. Add yeast and milk mixture and blend well. Divide dough into four equal parts. (Divide each again for smaller rolls.) Roll into thin oblongs and spread with nut mixture. Roll up, lightly sealing edges. Place on greased baking sheet and let rise until double. Bake at 350° F for 30 to 40 minutes.

Nut Filling
Ořechová nádivka

4 egg whites
1/4 cup sugar
1/8 teaspoon salt
1/2 lb. walnuts, ground

Beat egg whites until stiff. Combine sugar, salt, and walnuts, then fold into egg whites. Fill pastry.

A Tribute to Havel

"Havel devoted his life to the cause of human freedom. For years, Communism tried to crush him, and to extinguish his voice. But Havel, the playwright and the dissident, could not be silenced."

—British Prime Minister David Cameron

Apple *Bublanina*
Jablková bublanina

Arlene and Jerry Boddicker owned the Boddicker School of Music in the Czech Village. Arlene, who collected old-time band arrangements for the Boddicker band, also taught at Coe College and Mt. Mercy College in Cedar Rapids.

Arlene wrote "This recipe has been handed down for four generations on my mother's side of the family: Grandma Buresh to Grandma Hiroutek to Aunt Emma Zbanek to me."

3 quarts apples, peeled and sliced
1 1/2 cups sugar
1 teaspoon cinnamon or more
1/2 cup margarine or butter
2 eggs
2 cups milk
1 tablespoon sugar
2/3 teaspoon salt
2 cups flour
1 teaspoon baking powder

Place apples, 1 1/2 cups sugar, and cinnamon in large bowl. Mix and set aside. Melt margarine in 9"x13"x2" cake pan. Beat eggs until blended, add milk, 1 tablespoon sugar, and salt. Add flour and baking powder, making a thick batter, then pour over apples. Mix well and pour into cake pan, patting down firmly with back of spoon. As butter rises around edge of pan, dip up with spoon and spread over top of batter. Bake at 350° F for 1 hour and 15 minutes or until apples are golden. Serve warm or cold with whipped cream or ice cream. Serves 18.

Cherry *Bublanina*
Třešňová bublanina

Arlene Boddicker was given this recipe by her cousin, Agnes Konicek.

1/2 cup butter
1/2 cup sugar
3 eggs, separated
1 cup flour
1/2 teaspoon baking powder
pinch of salt
1 quart cherries (fresh, canned, or frozen), pitted, well drained

Cream together butter and sugar. Beat egg yolks until lemon colored. Add butter and sugar, beat until fluffy. Sift flour, baking powder, and salt together, then add to butter mixture. Beat egg whites until stiff and fold into batter slowly. Pour into greased 12" x 8" pan. Sprinkle cherries over top of the batter, do not mix. Bake at 450° F for 15 minutes.

A Poppy Seed Story

Paul Engle, the late noted American poet and writer, remembers that the Cedar Rapids Czechs were great wine makers. During Prohibition, they made even more. When he was a newsboy selling the Cedar Rapids *Gazette*, many of the newsboys were Czech, and they all enjoyed buying poppy seed kolaches at the Sykora bakery. "My mother did not want me to eat any poppy seed kolaches so that I would not acquire the opium habit. Naturally, I ate every one I could get my hands on. To this day, I have still not acquired the opium habit."

Divine Crullers
Boží milosti

M. Melvina Svec of Cedar Rapids remembered that these crullers have also been called Listí *(leaves) and* Křapáče *(crispies).*

1 egg
1 1/3 cups flour
1 tablespoon water
fat for deep frying

Combine egg and water, beating well. Add flour as needed until dough is similar to noodle dough. Amount of flour will vary with the size of the egg. Turn dough onto cloth or board and knead using rest of flour. Cut dough into 3 or 4 chunks. Roll out each piece as thin as possible, cut into pieces 2" to 3" across—squares, rectangles, triangles or any shapes to use the dough. Cut a diagonal slash in each piece. To test if fat is hot enough, drop a sample piece in; it should rise to the surface at once. As pieces are dropped into the fat, push fork through the slash to keep it open. When the slash is lightly brown, turn the piece over. Two forks may be helpful as one must work fast. Lift pieces onto brown paper to drain. When cooled, sprinkle with powdered sugar if served at once. Otherwise store in tight container and sugar them just before serving. Makes about 2 dozen. They enlarge during frying. This recipe does not include milk, cream, flavoring, salt, or butter.

Divine Crullers (with cream)
Boží milosti

Irma and John Kadlec worked together in a car distributorship in Czech Village for many years.

4 egg yolks, well beaten
4 tablespoons heavy cream
2 tablespoons sugar
1 egg white, beaten stiff
2 tablespoons rum or whiskey
1/8 teaspoon salt
1 3/4 to 2 cups flour

Beat egg yolks, cream, and sugar until well blended. Fold in egg white and rum or whiskey. Add salt and 1 cup flour, mix well. Add remaining flour gradually, mixing until dough is stiff. Knead for a minute and roll out 1/8" thick. Cut into strips about 1 1/2" x 4". Slash edges and twist slightly. Drop into hot deep fat at 360° F and fry until golden brown. Drain and dust with powdered sugar. Makes about 3 dozen.

Fish scale apron, kroj, *from Blata, Bohemia is in the collection of the National Czech & Slovak Museum & Library, Cedar Rapids, Iowa*

Celestial Crusts
Boží milosti

Esther Hronik Klersey was born in the heart of Czech Village when board sidewalks and dirt roads were common, and that area is very dear to her. As with her father, music has been her life. Most notably she directed the Karla Masaryk Chorus (named for the wife of the first president of Czechoslovakia), which dressed in authentic Czech costumes and appeared with many celebrities. They also recorded for the "Voice of America."

3 eggs
3 teaspoons sugar
2 tablespoons butter or lard
1/2 egg shell of water or cream
dash of salt
flour

Mix eggs, sugar, butter, cream, salt, and enough flour to make a stiff dough (but not as stiff as for noodles). Work all ingredients into a smooth dough. On lightly floured board, roll dough very thin. Cut into 3" squares and prick with a fork several times.

Fry in deep fat, like doughnuts, until lightly browned on both sides. Remove from fat and drain on paper towel. Dust generously with powdered sugar. Makes about 3 dozen.

Cream Puffs and Filling
Odpalované těsto s nádivkou

Leona Melhus of Atkins, Iowa, came from a family of eight children and started working at twelve years of age.

1 cup water
1/2 cup butter or margarine
1 cup flour
4 eggs

Bring butter and water to a boil, add flour and cook until dough leaves sides of pan, about 1 minute. Remove from heat. Add eggs one at a time, beat thoroughly. Drop by tablespoonfuls on cookie sheet. Bake at 425° F for 20 minutes, then 325° F for 25 to 30 minutes. Makes 18. Cool before filling.

Filling:

2/3 cup sugar
1/2 teaspoon salt
2 1/2 teaspoons cornstarch
1 tablespoon flour
3 cups milk
3 eggs, separated
2 tablespoons butter
2 teaspoons vanilla

Mix sugar, salt, cornstarch, and flour, add milk and cook in double boiler until slightly thickened. Add small amount of hot mixture to egg yolks and return to hot mixture, cook until thick. Remove from heat and add vanilla and butter. Chill. Beat egg whites thick with 1 tablespoon sugar. Fold into cream mixture. Slice puffs horizontally and place a tablespoonful of filling into each.

Mother's Chocolate Fudge
Maminčino čokoládové fondán

Hedrika Konecny Benesh of Cedar Rapids writes of her mother, Mrs. Adolph (Anna) Vavara Konecny, *"Mother was born in Czechoslovakia and helped raise twin baby brothers after her mother's death. At the age of fourteen she came to Cedar Rapids, with the aid of an older brother who had come earlier, and worked in the Grand Hotel, where she met and married our father. They moved to a farm near Ely, where they raised practically everything they needed, and even made cheese and butter to sell. Dad cured and smoked hams and bacon for himself and for the neighbors. Mother would fry down pork, make* jaternice, jelita, *and also* presburt.

"Holiday dinners would always include roast duck or goose, sage dressing, sauerkraut, potato dumplings, and pumpkin pie. At Christmas there was houska, *a variety of cookies, as well as* bozi milosit. *There were always* kolaches, rohlicky, *and delicious chicken on Sunday. Rye bread was baked during the week, as well as pies. How she did it and took care of a large garden, helped with the harvest of the fields, washing, ironing, and all is hard to realize. Especially when you realize that all the water was carried in from the well and the firewood for the cookstove, too. But what delicious meals were served. Nuts and dried apples were more delicacies we had to nibble on. Mushrooms were also dried or canned for winter along with all the fruits and vegetables. Winter evenings would be spent reading or ladies got together to strip feathers. They enjoyed visiting while working and a lunch would always follow."*

2 cups brown sugar
1 cup heavy cream
3/4 cup corn syrup
2 squares bitter chocolate
pinch salt
1 cup (or more) black walnuts
1 teaspoon vanilla

Boil together the sugar, cream, corn syrup, salt, and chocolate, until a few drops form a soft ball when dropped in cold water. Remove from heat and cool. Add vanilla and beat. Add nuts and beat until stiff. Pour quickly into a buttered loaf cake pan. Let cool and cut into squares. Mother used plenty of nuts, probably 3 or 3 1/2 cups. This is not so sweet as most candies.

St. Vitus Cathedral, Prague

Cut-Out Cookies
Česko-slovenské vykrajované koláčky

Mrs. Joe (Evelyn Svoboda) Stejskal of Cedar Rapids has many memories of growing up on a farm. "The week of Christmas we would do Christmas baking. Dad would take us into the timber to cut our tree. We helped him cut it down and haul it on the horse-drawn sleigh. Decorations were from Czechoslovakia. We put clip candle holders on the tree...Christmas Eve we'd all stand around the tree and light wax candles...and watch them carefully while we sang Christmas songs."

1 cup butter
3/4 cup powdered sugar
4 egg yolks
3 tablespoons light cream
1/2 teaspoon salt
1 teaspoon vanilla or lemon extract
3 cups sifted flour

Cream butter and sugar. Beat in egg yolks, cream, salt, and flavoring. Gradually stir in flour then chill for 1 hour. Roll out on board sprinkled with equal parts of flour and powdered sugar. When about 1/4" thick, cut into desired shapes and place on ungreased cookie sheet. Bake at 350° F to 375° F about 12 minutes. Cool and frost with icing.

Icing:
2 egg yolks
1 tablespoon water
1/2 teaspoon flavoring
powdered sugar

Beat egg yolks and water. Add your choice of flavoring and enough powdered sugar to make spreading consistency. Frost cookies and top with chopped almonds or colored sugar.

Molasses-Ginger Bars
Perníky

M. Melvina Svec is the author of My Czech Word Book: ABC Color Book. *"Sweets were never an everyday item on the table at meals in Old Bohemia for the average family. Even kolaches were made for festive events."*

3/4 cup lard
1/2 cup sugar
1 cup molasses
1 egg
1/2 cup hot water
1 teaspoon soda
3 cups flour
1 teaspoon ginger
pinch salt

Cream lard and sugar together. Add molasses and blend, then add egg. Dissolve soda in hot water and let cool. Add flour, ginger, and salt alternately with soda water. Dough is rather stiff. Spread on well greased and floured 9" x 13" pan. Bake at 350° F for 20 to 25 minutes. Drizzle with thin powdered sugar frosting (powdered sugar and milk or cream beaten together) when removed from oven. Cool and cut into bars or squares.

Needle Art

Today, Czech embroidery is researched, preserved, and continued in earnest in sewing circles. At Holy Trinity Catholic Church at Heun, rural Clarkson, Nebraska, the 70-year-old Heun Ladies Guild meets monthly to socialize while making decorative pillow cases, table linens, and tea towels. Motifs used preserve the Czech language, such as days of the week and familiar greetings.

Christmas Pudding Candy
Vánoční pudink

Mrs. Stanley Rejcha of Beatrice, Nebraska, sent a recipe of her great grandmother's, which she makes in November to be ready for Christmas.

3 cups sugar
1 cup cream
1 tablespoon butter
1 teaspoon vanilla
1 lb. dates, cut up
1 lb. figs, cut up
1 lb. raisins
1 lb. shredded coconut
1 cup nuts, chopped

Cook sugar, cream, and butter to soft ball stage (234° F). Beat until creamy. Beat in vanilla, fruit, and nuts. Roll up like a cookie roll and wrap in a damp cloth, then in waxed paper, and put in a cool place to ripen. Cut in slices as needed.

Czech Garnets
České granáty

Barbara Sovern of Cedar Rapids received this recipe from Emily Polacek, wife of an owner of the Polacek Brothers Meat Market. Barbara's father had a meat business in Chicago and his customers included the Polacek Brothers.

1/2 lb. butter
1 cup sugar
2 egg yolks
2 cups flour
1 cup chopped nuts
1/2 cup raspberry or strawberry jam

Cream butter and sugar. Add egg yolks

and blend well. Add flour gradually, mixing thoroughly. Fold in chopped nuts. Grease 8" square pan and spoon in half of batter. Top with jam and spoon on rest of batter. Bake in 325° F oven for 1 hour. When cool, cut in small squares. Makes 3 dozen cookies.

Apple Fritters
Jablkové smaženky

Helen Sysel Kupka, Crete, Nebraska: "My father had an orchard of various kinds of apples. We frequently made Apple Fritters. Many cooks used lard instead of butter for frying. Present day oil for frying would be good too."

3 or 4 firm apples
powdered sugar
2 eggs, beaten
1 teaspoon butter, melted
1 tablespoon milk
1 tablespoon sugar
pinch of salt
flour

Peel the apples, then slice them crosswise about 1/3" thick. Carefully remove cores. Sprinkle with powdered sugar, set aside. Mix eggs, butter, milk, sugar, salt, and enough flour to make a thin batter. Dip apple slices individually and fry in hot butter until tender and light brown.

Havel Advice

"Anyone who takes himself too seriously always runs the risk of looking ridiculous; anyone who can consistently laugh at himself does not."

—*Václav Havel*

Sweet Popcorn
Sladká pražená kukuřice

Fern Kaplan Fackler, Cedar Rapids, Iowa. Leona Netolicky Kaplan submitted an alternate method of preparation.

"This recipe has been enjoyed by members of our family and the Netolicky family for many years. When cream was readily available, the first recipe was used. Now when we are more apt to have butter or margarine on hand, the second recipe is easier to use. Our children have always loved this popcorn and delight in experimenting with coloring the syrup—sometimes purple, gray, and colors that are indescribable! We always make it at Christmas time and color some red and some green. We often used pastel colored sweet popcorn in May baskets."

Method 1:
1/2 cup cream
1 cup sugar
4 quarts popcorn

Bring cream and sugar to a boil and simmer for 3 to 5 minutes. Add food coloring if desired. Pour over 4 quarts unsalted popped corn and mix.

Method 2:
3 tablespoons butter or margarine
3 tablespoons water
1 cup sugar
4 quarts popcorn

Bring butter, water, and sugar to a boil and simmer for 3 minutes. Add food coloring if desired. Pour over popped corn and mix.

Sugar Cookies
Česko-slovenské cukrové koláčky

Lenore Topinka, Cedar Rapids, Iowa

1 cup margarine
1 cup shortening
1 cup powdered sugar
1 cup granulated sugar
2 eggs
1 teaspoon vanilla
1 teaspoon soda
1 teaspoon cream of tartar
4 cups flour

Cream margarine, shortening, and sugars. Add eggs and vanilla. Stir in remaining ingredients. Roll dough into balls about the size of walnuts and roll the balls in some powdered sugar. Place on a greased cookie sheet 2 inches apart. Bake at 375° F for 12 minutes. Makes 6 dozen.

This Czech lead crystal vase was presented to the National Czech & Slovak Museum & Library by Václav Havel, president of the Czech Republic, at the opening of the museum in 1995.

And More

Cottage Cheese
Jak dělat tvaroh

Mrs. Krejci shares her cottage cheese recipe, "We ate the dry curds softened with rich milk or cream. Sometimes we added chives or onion tops. The pigs got the whey!"

Whole milk was allowed to set for 6 or 8 hours, then the cream was skimmed off and the milk used for cottage cheese. A two gallon stoneware crock was filled and set on the back of the cookstove—very little heat. The crock was covered with just any old lid. It remained there until curds developed, maybe 8 hours, maybe 24. We used a wooden spoon to stir and test. When it was ready, it was poured into a white flour sack. The the whey was drained off and the curds were forced into a corner of the sack and hung on the clothes line to dry for 6 to 8 hours.

Mushroom Fritters
Houbové smaženky

Mrs. Lumir Kopecky, Cedar Rapids

1/2 lb. mushrooms, chopped
1 tablespoon butter or margarine
2 eggs, separated
2 tablespoons milk
1 cup flour
1 teaspoon baking powder
1/2 teaspoon salt
pinch of paprika
frying oil
cream sauce

Sauté the mushrooms lightly in butter. In separate bowl beat the 2 egg yolks with milk and blend in flour, baking powder, salt, and paprika. Beat the batter until smooth and add mushrooms. Beat the egg whites until stiff and fold into the batter. Drop by spoonfuls into hot oil and fry on both sides until golden brown. Serve with cream sauce.

Homemade Wine
Domácí víno

Evelyn Rainosek Vacera of Bellaire, Texas, grew up by the Colorado River in La Grange, Texas, on the farm of her grandparents. "My uncles would go to the river and pick the grapes when they were ripe and make this wine. I use it for cooking most of the time."

8 cups grapes
4 cups sugar
1 gallon boiling water

Take a clean 1 gallon glass jar with a good lid. Use wild, ripe grapes, or grapes you have in your area. Wash well; fill jar with grapes and sugar. Add boiling water to within 1 inch of the top. Tighten lid and leave to ferment till grape seeds, skins, etc. drop to the bottom. Then it is ready.

Tomáš Masaryk
First President of Czechoslovakia

Stamps for collectors at Sykora's Bakery, Cedar Rapids, Iowa

Listing of Recipes

Prague marionette sculpture

About the Author
Pat Martin

Photo by Mel Holubar

Pat Martin (left), author, is not Czech and does not wear an authentic kroj. *However, she enjoys wearing this authentic apron from Chodovia, Czech Republic, with an American style skirt and blouse.*

NCSML Guild member Cyndi Kula O'Brien, who created her kroj, *is standing with Pat.*

Pat and Cyndi were in the Houby Days Parade and participated in a Parade of Kroje, sponsored by Czech Heritage Association in Cedar Rapids.

Pat Martin was the first Czech Village Coordinator (1977–86), working within the Czech Village Association, Czech Heritage Foundation, and Czech Fine Arts groups. These Czechs updated their Village in Cedar Rapids, with sidewalkscapes, landscaping, building design, and renovations. Pat, a 100 percent Irish woman whose birth name is McConville, is a volunteer with the Guild of NCSML (National Czech & Slovak Museum & Library). A past Guild president, she is a museum docent who enjoys giving tours for children. A former high school language arts teacher, Pat is a mother, widow, and grandmother. She seeks to build partnerships with others to help preserve their cultural heritages. Penfield books she has written include *Prague: Saints of the Charles Bridge, Czech Wit and Wisdom, Czechoslovak Culture, Czech and Slovak Touches, The Czech Book,* and this book *Czech Touches*

Acknowledgements: A special thank you to Dave Muhlena, librarian, Diana Baculis, director of marketing NCSML; Bob Stone, Carolyn and Mel Holubar, Guenter and Donna Merkle, and all persons named in text of this and earlier editions and others who contributed essays, recipes, and photographs to this book. **Editors:** Dwayne and Joan Liffring-Zug Bourret, Melinda Bradnan, Miriam Canter, Esther Feske, John Johnson, Ann Kloubec, Whitney Pope, David Wright, Deb Schense, and Connie Schnoebelen.

A Final Word

"None of us know all the potentialities that slumber in the spirit of the population, or all the ways in which that population can surprise us when there is the right interplay of events."

—*Václav Havel*